In Defense of All God's Children

The Life and Ministry of Bishop Christopher Senyonjo

Memoirs

of

The Rt. Rev. Dr. Christopher Senyonjo
Retired Bishop of West Buganda Diocese in Uganda

Morehouse Publishing
NEW YORK

This book is dedicated to my father, Erika Kapere,
and my mother, Maria Nosianta Nakalyango Terugwa.

Morehouse Publishing, 19 East 34th Street, New York, NY 10016

Morehouse Publishing is an imprint of Church Publishing Incorporated. www.churchpublishing.org

Cover photo by David Tiklun, Amsterdam, 2015
Cover design by Jennifer Kopec, 2Pug Design
Typeset by Rose Design

Library of Congress Cataloging-in-Publication Data

Names: Senyonjo, Christopher, author.
Title: In defense of all God's children : the life and ministry of Bishop
  Christopher Senyonjo / memoirs of the Rt. Rev. Dr. Christopher Senyonjo.
Description: New York : Morehouse Publishing, 2016. | Includes
  bibliographical references.
Identifiers: LCCN 2015050050 (print) | LCCN 2016006719 (ebook) | ISBN
  9780819232434 (pbk.) | ISBN 9780819232441 (ebook)
Subjects: LCSH: Senyonjo, Christopher. | Church of
  Uganda—Bishops—Biography. | Uganda—Church history. | Sexual
  orientation—Religious aspects—Christianity. | Homosexuality—Religious
  aspects—Christianity.
Classification: LCC BX5700.8.Z8 S46 2016 (print) | LCC BX5700.8.Z8 (ebook) |
  DDC 283.092—dc23
LC record available at http://lccn.loc.gov/2015050050

Printed in the United States of America

Contents

౸

Foreword

JESUS IS THE CENTER OF THE CHRISTIAN STORY. The son
of poor, rural Jews, Jesus was dedicated to those on the margins.
His chosen disciples were a motley crew of twelve who had little
to offer by way of political power. His miracles addressed bodily
needs: hunger, thirst, sickness. Jesus's allegiance to the oppressed
was blasphemy to the tyrannical empire, which realized the radical
nature of his message. To tell disenfranchised people that their lives
and their stories matter is to undermine the systems of exploitation
on which empires depend for their survival. Jesus modeled change,
and commissioned his followers to do the same.

There are a handful of figures that we revere for so thoroughly
inhabiting the example of Jesus—Tutu, Tubman, King, Gandhi.
Certainly, the Rt. Rev. Disani Christopher Senyonjo belongs in
such company. Deep and sustaining change only happens in our
world when faithful people stand up and speak truth in the face
of power against enormous odds, and Bishop Senyonjo has done
precisely that.

Bishop Senyonjo has been a strong and consistent advocate for
LGBTQ rights in his home country of Uganda, and was awarded
the Clinton Global Citizen Award for his work. He has spoken out
against the criminalization of homosexuality and the violence that
LGBTQ people face, and faced persecution from his diocese for
taking such a revolutionary position. His story has since been told
in the documentary film *God Loves Uganda*. He has spent decades
counseling LGBTQ people, telling many of them for the first time
that they are loved and celebrated. Most of all, Bishop Senyonjo
is unwavering in his commitment to the oppressed, a Christian

minister in the prophetic tradition who continues to risk his professional and personal safety to advocate for those in need.

God Loves Uganda put Bishop Senyonjo on an international stage, bringing him to the attention of renowned leaders, policy makers, intellectuals, and activists. However, his work started long before the film's release. This book gives us an intimate glimpse into the life that shaped Bishop Senyonjo's powerful ministry. How lucky we are for it.

I am grateful that Union Theological Seminary played a role in Bishop Senyonjo's development. We are very proud to have him as an alumnus because he so thoroughly embodies the Union spirit. Union Theological Seminary is a graduate school of theology established in 1836 by founders "deeply impressed by the claims of the world upon the church." At Union, we prepare women and men for committed lives of service to the church, academy, and society, fostering intellectual and academic excellence, a social justice consciousness, and compassionate wisdom. Now eight years into my tenure as president, I am still amazed by the courage and diversity of our beloved seminary. Union leaders shine, and Bishop Senyonjo is our proof positive. We lift up his example to our students all the time.

In 2014, we welcomed him back to our campus as a scholar-in-residence, along with his wife, Mary. During his residency, Bishop Senyonjo reflected on his life of ministry and wrote the first draft of the memoirs you are about to read. It's impressive to see a person who can one week stand in the corridors of high power in Uganda and the next week stand in the boardrooms of Wall Street, all the while demonstrating a fidelity to his ministerial identity. Wherever he finds himself, Bishop Senyonjo remains a man of deep faith, grounded in compassion and humility. May God continue to bless him.

Serene Jones
President of the Faculty, Union Theological Seminary &
Johnston Family Professor for Religion and Democracy

Preface

I AM THANKFUL FOR THE LONG LIFE God has granted me thus far and for any extra earthly life in store for me. In my lifetime, I have discovered that loving and worshipping God has given my life purpose. God's love for me and others compels me to want to serve him and my fellow human beings for as long as I am able.

I am blessed to be an alumnus of the Union Theological Seminary (UTS) in New York City; I received my master of divinity (MDiv) and master of sacred theology (STM) degrees in 1966 and 1967, respectively. The rigorous theological training I received at Union has enabled me to align my faith with understanding. I am convinced that God is a God of order, reason, and understanding and not of confusion. Our God is still creating out of disorder. It is by God's providence that I returned to Union Theological Seminary—forty-seven years after my graduation—to write my memoirs.

I am particularly grateful to Union's president, Dr. Serene Jones, for inviting me and my wife to participate in the life of this wonderful seminary again. My wife, Mary, is with me, supporting me as I study, communicate, and write my memoirs in the surroundings in which we both lived when Joseph, our first child, was conceived. Joseph was born at Women's Hospital (St. Luke's Hospital) in New York City while I studied at Union.

I am also grateful to the seminary's board of governors, its administration, and support staff who ensured that our lodging and accommodation were conducive to happy memories and to productive writing.

I am grateful to Joseph for his support during this period. Soon after my return to Union to write these memoirs, I fell sick before Mary joined me. Joseph took me to St. Luke's Hospital and checked on me for the three days I was hospitalized there. It was a godsend that Joseph, a longtime New York City resident, was available to assist Mary and me with navigating the big metropolis for the six months as I worked on these memoirs while in residence at UTS.

I

My Formative Years

ON DECEMBER 8, 1931, I WAS BORN to Ms. Maria Nosianta Nakalyango Terugwa Mukulu-Abula-Awawe and Mr. Erika Kapere. My father named me "Senyonjo," an Egret (Nyonyi-Nyange) clan name from Buganda in Uganda. In Buganda, clans, which are extended ancestral family lineages, are critical identifiers. Each clan is symbolized by a totem, normally an animal, bird, fish, or other object which is considered sacred and inedible for clan members. Each of the clans has a set of male and female names that are exclusive to it. Before one courts a love interest, one must know the beloved's clan, for clan members are considered brothers and sisters. Thus clan marriages are exogenous; that is, one has to marry from outside his or her clan. Traditionally, one cannot even marry someone from his or her mother's clan, as that is considered taboo—like marrying your maternal aunt or uncle.

The name "Senyonjo" signifies cleanness, perhaps deriving from the clan's totem: an egret, an immaculately white bird. I understand that my father chose that name because he valued cleanness and wished that I live a clean life. My father might have given me another name such as "Kyeyune," which means "follow it up immediately." He did not. I feel that the name "Senyonjo" has shaped my life as I put "love" first of all other pursuits in the universe. Love is the cleanest concept that I can ever imagine in this life and thereafter.

I was my mother's firstborn child. Her two other children were my younger siblings: sister, Meresiane, and brother, Langton; respectively four and nine years younger than me.

On the other hand, I was the youngest of my father's three children. I had two elder half-brothers: Ananias Kyeyune and Yokana Senyonga. Although we did not belong to one mother, my brothers and I grew up caring and respecting each other. Ananias and Yokona died leaving no children. I chose to name two of my grandchildren "Kyeyune" and "Senyonga" in memory of my two childless brothers.

My mother was an intelligent and loving disciplinarian who taught me to respect not only my siblings, but all people. She did not tolerate discrimination of any kind. She also served as my home kindergarten teacher.

Before I enrolled in school, my mother had already taught me the alphabet of my mother tongue, Luganda, the native language of the Buganda kingdom that is located within Uganda. While instructing me, my mother tolerated neither laziness nor absentmindedness. Thanks to her strict discipline, I developed a voracious interest in reading as a way to learn about the world. Even now, at eighty-three, I take great pleasure in reading a wide variety of books and newspapers.

Even though I was a little boy, I vividly remember Mr. Yafesi Lwanga, a road inspector and family friend, suggesting to my mother that I was old enough, at five, to join the local primary school at Sinde. Mr. Lwanga had seen me reading the *Mateka Elementary Book* but observed that I could not write; my mother had neither skill nor implements to enable her to teach me how to write. Aware of her limitations, my mother gladly accepted Mr. Lwanga's suggestion.

I remember my mother as a brave woman. Before the establishment of game reserves, wild animals would sometimes roam villages looking for prey. One day, when I was still a child, a lion attacked my mother's goats, but she made such a hullabaloo—shouting and gesturing—that the lion dropped its prey and fled as villagers rushed to help.

And when I was about five years old, a thug with a machete broke into our home. Instinctively, my seven-year-old nephew,

Wilson Lubuka, and I hid under the bed. My fearless mother somehow managed to grab the man's testicles, squeezing them so hard that the thief fled, writhing in pain. Needless to say, he left his machete behind!

My mother remained a staunch Catholic throughout her life, despite my position as bishop in the Anglican Church. One time, when she came to visit us at Kako, I drove her, along with Joseph, to Kitovu Catholic Cathedral a few miles away for Mass. Joseph fondly related that the nuns at Bishop Adrian Ddungu's residence entertained them well, and that the distinguished bishop personally drove the two of them back to our home in his Volkswagen Beetle.

Near the end of her life, when she was very sick, my mother confided in me that she knew she was about to die. But before I could take her to hospital, she asked of me one favor: summon a Catholic priest to administer unction to her. I brought the priest as she requested. As I drove her to the hospital in Kampala, she told me that she was only going for my sake, as she did not want me to live with any regrets. The day after her admission at the hospital, she died peacefully at the age of seventy-five.

My father was a hardworking man. He spoke fluent English, a rare skill in Uganda at the time. This fluency served him well when he served as a chef to the British colonial governor at Entebbe. I remember him fondly calling me "Nyonjo," short for Senyonjo.

One day, during my childhood, when I was weak with pneumonia, my heel accidentally got stuck in my father's bicycle spokes as he transported me for treatment. The spokes chewed a chunk off my heel. Fortunately the bicycle stopped before the spokes could pierce my right leg. By God's grace, I healed without getting tetanus.

When I was ten, a length of sticky sharp grass got stuck on my arm as I played; it left a permanent cross-shaped scar. In my fertile imagination, I often wonder if that was a sign that God would call me to follow Christ's example to bear the cross in God's service.

My father took a keen interest in my studies: whenever I returned from school, he would ask me to narrate what I had learned that day; in turn I would eagerly recite Bible, hygiene, English, and arithmetic lessons to him. He was proud of my excellent academic performance, but he felt compelled to move me to another school due to other parents' envious remarks. He considered it ominous when they suggested that he should contribute a lion's share to the school's maintenance as I was purportedly the "pillar" of the school—he feared that jealous parents could harm me and perhaps even endanger my life.

Out of caution, my father asked his relative, Mr. Douglas Kyeyune, a teacher at Bukomero Primary School, to enroll me at his school. In 1942, at ten years old, I left home and went to stay with Mr. Kyeyune. I found him to be smart, kind, quick-witted, and a very good footballer. In 1943, Mr. Kyeyune and I moved when he was transferred from Bukomero Primary School to Nsangi Primary School. While at Nsangi, Mr. Kyeyune married his fiancée, Ms. Miriam Nabutto, who became like a mother to me. In fact, she was so kind and caring that I endeavored to please her at all costs.

Mrs. Kyeyune is today still fond of telling stories about me. For instance, she recalls that one day, I was asked to slaughter a chicken for dinner. I was horrified, but I complied under pressure, cutting the chicken's throat with my eyes closed!

She also recounts a time, during her first pregnancy, when she sent me on an errand to buy beef. When I discovered that butcheries in the neighborhood had already depleted their stock, I walked from Nsangi to Nalukolongo town—eight miles each way—to buy the beef as I could not dare disappoint her.

In 1944, Mr. Kyeyune was transferred from Nsangi Primary school to Nakanyonyi Primary School, in Kyaggwe County, and I accompanied him. That same year, in April, a cobra, hanging on a tree branch, spat on my father as he returned home from his farm at Kanzira. At first he did not think much of it, but his face, neck, throat, and chest soon began to swell. He passed away within only two days. Unfortunately, in those days there were no easy means of communication in rural Uganda, thus the news of my father's death reached us after his burial. I visited his grave soon afterward. I confess to thinking that my family had not made enough effort to reach me before the burial. Not being present for my father's burial left a wound in my heart that has never completely healed.

Following my father's death, my aunt, Yudesi Nanyonga, asked Mr. Kyeyune to let her take care of me. In 1945, I relocated from Nakanyonyi, in Kyaggwe county, to Kitti, in Kyadondo county, to stay with my aunt and her husband, Mr. Bernardo Bamwera. I enrolled in primary five (fifth grade) at Wampewo Primary School, six miles from my aunt's house. To attenuate the distance, my aunt gave me a bicycle to ride to the school. My aunt, an intelligent and business-minded woman, showed me how to prepare banana pancakes, which she encouraged me to sell at school.

While at Wampewo Primary School, I met the late Hannington Kintu, a child from a well-to-do family, who would become a lifelong friend. Hannington and I were grade 5 classmates, even though he was a year older than me. I liked him because he was quiet and gentlemanlike. He was also a clever and hardworking student, so we studied together. Hannington's clan, the leopard, was also my mother's clan. As per Buganda culture, I referred to him as my maternal uncle. Hannington and I became so close that we were like brothers; I often went with him at his invitation to visit his parents in Kamuli. Our families became intertwined.

In 1946, I sat for Primary Leaving Examinations, which qualified me to join Junior Secondary School. The headmaster of Wampewo Primary School, Mr. Yosamu Kijjambu, a smart, disciplined, and father-like figure, worked hard to ensure that his students performed well. As I approached graduation, Mr. Kijjambu encouraged me to apply to King's College Budo, "the Eton of Uganda," for secondary school enrollment. It was a somewhat intimidating prospect, as the school's students were chosen from among the brightest pupils in the country, and many came from well-to-do families. Even if I were lucky enough to be admitted, I wondered how my aunt and I could afford to pay the school's expensive tuition and fees. Nevertheless, Mr. Kijjambu had great faith in me. He was convinced that my academic performance would pave the way.

When the examination results returned, I was informed that I had done well and had won a scholarship to King's College Budo (KCB).The scholarship would cover all tuition and fees. I thought I was dreaming!! Hannington also performed well and joined me at KCB.

Mr. Ssemugoma, the KCB assistant headmaster, told me that the scholarship would cover my educational expenses as long as I kept up good grades. Fortunately, I managed to maintain good grades throughout my six years at Budo, from 1947 until 1952, when I completed senior secondary school.

I performed well in both the arts and the sciences, but I particularly excelled in the sciences. Biology, chemistry, physics, and mathematics fascinated me because they gave me insights into causes and effects of various phenomena. While at Budo, I served as a library monitor, a position which gave me ample opportunity to pursue my hobby of reading astronomy books. I was greatly intrigued by celestial bodies—the planets, stars, comets, and meteors. Astronomy also humbled me as I realized that we humans (and our planet) are relatively minuscule creatures in God's vast universe.

In the arts, I particularly enjoyed history and religious knowledge. In fact, one of my best subject performances at Budo was in Mr. John Barlow's religious knowledge examination, which I passed with a perfect score.

Apart from Mr. Barlow's classes, I also remember Mr. Frank Kalimuzo's history lessons, particularly regarding the evolution of early man; living in caves, using stone tools, and discovering fire. Mr. Kalimuzo, an exciting and captivating teacher, later went for further studies in the United Kingdom at Oxford and at University College of Aberystwyth, where he graduated with an honors degree in economics. He then served in several high-profile civil service positions and later on became a distinguished chancellor of Makerere University. Sadly, he was murdered by Idi Amin, who suspected him of links with Obote, whom he had served as permanent secretary.

After secondary school, my ambition was to join Makerere University College to study medicine. In 1953, I was admitted to Makerere University's Faculty of Science to do medicine. The prospect of joining the university to study medicine excited me, but I also looked forward to partaking in big city life that Kampala, where the university is located, offered. Unfortunately, I got so swept up in merrymaking that I did not concentrate on my studies. I mistakenly thought that I had plenty of time; I could relax during the first year of medical school and begin serious study in subsequent years, but there would be no subsequent years; I failed and was discontinued.

In 1954, as I reflected about my future, I found a teaching job at Luwule Secondary School (1954–1957), where I taught English, mathematics, and health sciences.

While at Luwule, I fell in love with Jennet Nantale, a beautiful, intelligent girl, who lived with her widowed mother. Jennet and I were both relatively young at twenty and twenty-three years old, respectively. After a relatively short time dating, Jennet came to live with me. Her mother consented, although Jennet and I were not legally married. During the three years that Jennet and I lived together, we had two children: Moses Baluduka Sembusi and Night Nabulime. Unfortunately, in the course of those three years, Jennet and I also frequently clashed due to mutual jealousies and unfounded suspicions. One day, when Jennet returned home at 10 o'clock in the evening after visiting her mother, I accused her of unfaithfulness; predictably, a bad violent fight ensued, resulting in the end of our relationship. I continued to support our two children, whom she kept custody of. Jennet later happily married and bore more children.

In 1958, I was transferred to Seeta Secondary School. That same year, at the age of twenty-seven, I decided to look for someone to marry. I vowed that this time the marriage would be officially sanctified by the church. I sought God's guidance in the matter. As I seriously pondered marriage, an uncle by the name of Gershom Bifamuntunzi suggested that I visit him in Masaka District. While there he introduced me to several attractive girls. Among them was Ruth Nakanwagi, a beautiful, slender girl from a respectable family. When I saw Ruth, I fell for her. After a period of courtship, Ruth consented to marry me.

In 1959, shortly after Easter, Ruth and I were married at Misanvu Anglican Church.

After the wedding, we stayed for one week at Mr. George Mwesezi's home, after which we returned to my house at Kiwugo, in Mukono District. After another week of rest, I returned to my teaching job at Seeta Mwanyangiri College, about three miles from our home.

Ruth, who was full of vigor and life, stayed home. On the third day, after my return to my teaching job, Ruth went to tend to our sweet potato garden. Tragically, a poisonous snake hiding among the leaves bit her leg. On receiving the news, I rushed home in panic. I found Ruth in pain; she confided to me that she was scared.

I rushed her to the nearest medical center at Mukono, but her condition worsened. We transferred her to Mulago Hospital in Kampala, but she died the same day, with me at her bedside. Ruth and I had been married for only seventeen days; the tragedy was almost too much for me to bear.

I am grateful to Dr. Mohammed Kasasa, a friend and classmate at both Budo and Makerere University, who supported me throughout the whole ordeal. He hardly spoke a word, but his presence strengthened me.

Ultimately, only Scripture consoled me:

> No testing has overtaken you that is not common to everyone. God is faithful, and he will not let you be tested beyond your strength, but with the testing he will also provide the way out so that you may be able to endure it. (1 Cor. 10:13)

I had first heard this verse while at King's College Budo when the Rev. Richard Drown, who was our chaplain and Bible studies teacher, read it to us. Its words flashed through my mind at the very moment Ruth was pronounced dead. I understood then that through God's strength I could endure despite Ruth's tragic death.

After Ruth's burial, I returned to teaching at Seeta College. On August 9, 1959, while back at home in Kiwugo, I heard Mr. Edward Nsulo interpret the Gospel according to John (3:3):

> Jesus answered him, "Very truly, I tell you, no one can see the kingdom of God without being born from above."

On hearing the gospel, and with Mr. Nsulo's encouragement, I understood that salvation was the only means to the kingdom of God. I committed my life to Jesus Christ, and thus began my pilgrimage in the service of the Lord.

Seeking Further Studies

To further my commitment, I independently registered for A-level certificate examinations majoring in divinity, economics, and history.[1] I passed the examinations and was awarded the A-level certificate in 1960. Subsequently, I applied to Buwalasi Theological College in Mbale for the then newly introduced East Africa diploma in theology.

As I considered church ministry, I consulted my good friend, Hannington Kintu. I frankly told him that I was struggling with the idea of embarking on a path to priesthood. He was surprised and skeptical because for all the years he had known me, he had never heard me talk about becoming a minister in the church. But when I told him how God spoke to me at Ruth's deathbed, he

---

1. This is akin to American students independently studying for the GRE outside of a formal school environment.

wholeheartedly encouraged me to pursue God's call. In addition to Hannington's advice, I also sought my mother's advice. I was particularly concerned that a three-year absence, as I pursued theological studies in distant Mbale, would cause my mother hardship, as I could no longer offer her financial support. To my surprise, my mother categorically told me that she couldn't stand in the way of God: "If God has called you, you must go," she said.

Despite the support and encouragement, I was still full of doubt and trepidation. I knew my weaknesses. As a young boy, my ambition was not to become a minister of the church. Rather, I wanted to be either a medical doctor or a businessman. I felt that ministers were not remunerated well enough for the hard conditions in which they often served. Years later, one of my sons, David Muyanja, decided to study medicine at Makerere University. He is now the head of the Internal Medicine Department at Mengo Hospital, one of the major hospitals in Kampala. I am proud of his accomplishment and I thank God for his call to the medical ministry that had also been my dream.

The admission process to the ordination course required an interview and a recommendation from Canon Wampamba, the rural dean in charge of the Mukono parish church where I was a member. In fact, I was such an active member of the church that I read Scripture lessons to the congregation on Sundays. After screening me, Canon Wampamba recommended me to Bishop Leslie Brown for a final interview.

The bishop and his team that included Archdeacon Waibale asked me, among other questions: "Have you carefully considered the sacrifices that you have to make as a minister in the church?" I responded that I was ready for any eventualities, and that my well-being was in God's hands. On passing the interview, I was admitted into the inaugural diploma course at Buwalasi Theological College.

Even after my admission to Buwalasi, I continued to struggle with my decision to study theology. However, a divine revelation soon changed that: One night, in a particularly vivid dream, I saw a bright candle burning in front of me. I tried to blow it out, blowing very hard, but the candle would not go out. Out of the blue, a huge mound of soil appeared. I decided to extinguish the stubborn candle by completely burying it in the soil. To my amazement, the candle's flames burst out from it, as if sprinkled with gasoline. I could not put the flames out! I woke up suddenly.

My interpretation of the dream was that I could not put out the flame that God had lit in me; I could not stop God's calling. Only then did I surrender unconditionally to joining the ministry; I enrolled at Buwalasi Theological College (1961–1963).

In 1963, I graduated from Buwalasi with a diploma in theology. I was one of just two students in the class. My colleague, Enos Bagona, was a brilliant man from the Ankole Kingdom of Uganda. As the only two students in the course, Enos and I had the full attention of our teachers; we had to be constantly alert in class! In retrospect, I am grateful for the intense instruction and attention we received because as the pioneer students in Uganda of the East Africa diploma in theology, our success was critical since the two of us paved the way for other highly qualified young men to join church ministry ranks.

While at Buwalasi, I made many friends from other parts of Uganda. There were students from Gulu, Kitgum, Lira, Soroti, Mbale, Sebei, Madi-West Nile, Tororo, and Karamoja. Other than Enos and me, the rest of the students were pursuing a certificate in theology. My leadership skills were first honed at Buwalasi, when I campaigned and got elected "senior student," the equivalent of "head prefect" in other school settings. I served in that capacity for two of my three years at Buwalasi. I tried to be just and caring for all students without discrimination.

It was at Buwalasi that I first got to know the Rev. Janani Luwum, one of the instructors at the college, who greatly impressed me. He patiently guided me in my role as senior student. His guidance was deeply appreciated, as some students were stubborn and prone to violence. The Rev. Luwum struck me as a just, nonprejudiced, upright man of God. Later, when I became a bishop, I got to work with Janani again when he was enthroned as the archbishop of the Church of Uganda, Rwanda, and Boga-Zaire.

The Rev. Eric Hutchison, another instructor at Buwalasi, had a profound influence on the course of my life. He was like my Gamaliel, the great teacher that Paul talks about in the Acts of the Apostles. Rev. Hutchison's deep and charismatic teaching of the Old Testament, history, and theology transfixed me. His discussion of hubris in the context of the Tower of Babel and of God creating *ex nihilo* (creating out of nothing) deeply fascinated me.

Today, when I reflect on the phenomenon of the Big Bang, I recall Rev. Hutchison's discussion of God creating *ex nihilo*. He also taught us that God loves us with steadfast love (*hesed*), and that we were created in God's own image. Nonetheless, he warned that we should be careful not to make God in our own image. This caution is still pertinent to religious institutions today that imagine themselves infallible embodiments of God's word. God is transcendent—he eludes our imagination and understanding. What we know about God is partial, and only by revelation.

The Rev. Eric Hutchinson would become more than a mentor to me. In due course, we became such good friends that he asked me to be a godparent to one of his children, Mark.

Toward the end of 1963, Enos Bagona and I successfully graduated with our diplomas in theology and were ordained deacons in the Anglican Church of Uganda shortly thereafter.

Toward the end of my second year at Buwalasi, and three years after Ruth's death, I sought marriage again. At the beginning of 1963, Mr. Edward Nsulo and I prayed to God to help me find a suitable partner. This was not an idle matter, because as a minister in the church, I had to search for a young woman who was a firm believer in the living God.

On a mission, Mr. Nsulo and I visited Ndejje Teacher Training College, where I spotted a beautiful girl, whose name was Mary Kyebakola. Not only was she beautiful, but she was also smart and kind. I fell in love with her at first sight. When I found out that Mary was also a devout Christian, I assiduously courted her. It was not easy to win her affection, but I remembered the English saying: "A faint heart has never won a fair lady!" So I persisted, and ultimately won her love.

Shortly after my graduation from Buwalasi, Mary and I got married at Namirembe Cathedral on December 28, 1963. Two weeks earlier, I had been ordained deacon at the same cathedral.

During our honeymoon, Mary and I visited several places. First, we stayed at Rev. Kezekiya Kalule's residence in Jungo for one week. We were then hosted by the Rev. Absalom Omojong

Wedding day photograph of Christopher and Mary Senyonjo, on December 28, 1963.

at his home at Buwalasi for a few days. From Buwalasi we proceeded to Limuru and Nairobi in neighboring Kenya. The Hon.
Elijah Agar, a member of Kenya's Parliament, and my former
classmate at Budo, warmly welcomed us. He gave us a nice tour
of Nairobi and of Kenya's parliamentary building. On our way
back to Uganda, we stayed with a friend in Nakuru. While there,
we were awed by flamingoes and many other beautiful birds at
Lake Nakuru. It was a happy honeymoon; we are grateful to all
the friends that made it possible.

After our return from our honeymoon, I was posted to work
with Rev. Asa Byara, the managing director and priest in charge of
"The Greater Kampala Project." As a young deacon, my task was to
assist the Rev. Byara and his team in opening up worship centers in
various Kampala locations. We opened centers in all sorts of places,
including bars, restaurants, and marketplaces. For instance, we
negotiated with bar owners to let us conduct prayer services in their
premises on Sunday mornings when there would be no clients.

Such locations enabled us to offer pastoral care to people in
Naguru, Ntinda, Bukoto, Namuwongo, Kiswa, Makerere Kivulu,
and Wandegeya. Our modus operandi was to go where people were
rather than to wait for them to come to us. Proper churches would
follow later. My major assignment was to minister at the Ntinda
and Bukoto church centers.

The Rev. Asa Byara and I were pioneers in the use of interim
worship structures, such as the "biwempe" recently adopted by Pen-
tecostal churches in Uganda, prior to building permanent structures.

My Time at Union Theological Seminary (1964-1967)

It is a great blessing that I was granted the opportunity to write my
memoirs while in residence at Union Theological Seminary (UTS),
the institution that has had the greatest impact on my theological
thinking, and which helped prepare me for ministry in the church.

The Rev. Eric Hutchison, my teacher at Buwalasi and a UTS alumnus, recommended that I pursue further theological training at Union. He had thoroughly prepared me for more advanced theological training; he was also convinced that UTS was the best seminary to which I could apply. Following his advice, I applied to Union for a bachelor of divinity (BD), now the (MDiv) degree. Fortunately, I was admitted and offered a scholarship that enabled me to attend.

I recall this first trip to the United States in July 1964 as an exciting experience. I felt separated from my wife and was lonely on this long flight from Entebbe, Uganda, to J.F.K. Airport in New York City. On my arrival in New York, I was astounded by the skyscrapers, the large cars, and the wide highways, the likes of which I had not seen anywhere in Africa. I wished Mary was with me to share and marvel at the glamour and wonders of the new world. She was to join me sometime later the following year.

When I left Uganda, Mary was in the third trimester of her first pregnancy. Sadly, in September 1964, our firstborn, a baby girl we named Kutesa, which means "God's will," died at birth. She was buried in our land at Kiti in Kyadondo County.

By God's grace, Mary withstood the shock of the loss and recovered her strength. She fondly remembers that our bishop, the Rt. Rev. Dr. Leslie Brown, prayed for her not to lose heart, and that he beseeched God to bless us with more children.

Mary arrived in New York in June 1965 after we had been separated for a year, but found me hospitalized. In May 1965, after I had successfully completed my first year at Union, I fell sick with pneumonia and was admitted to St. Luke's Hospital. I was discharged one month after Mary's arrival. I could not take summer courses in Hebrew during my recuperation. I was not used to the pollution that was in the air of New York City, the main cause of contracting pneumonia. I thank God that I fully recovered and continued my studies the following academic year without a hitch.

Prior to coming to New York, Eric Hutchison had already referred me to the Rev. Dr. Hugh McCandless, his former rector at the Church of Epiphany in New York City. Thus, on arriving in New York, among my first priorities was to find the Rev. Dr. McCandless and to locate his church. I located the church on the New York City map, and took a bus there. I was greatly impressed by the warm welcome that Rev. McCandless accorded me. Here I was, a young and green deacon from rural Africa, being received unreservedly by a distinguished rector of a church in New York City!

At Union, my professor of speech was instrumental in helping me learn to be articulate and audible. New Testament Professor John Knox and Systematic Theology Professors John Macquarie and Day Williams were also great teachers. Professor Day Williams impressed on us that God is always creating. He is both primordial and consequential.

As Jesus put it, "My Father is still working" (John 5:17). The implications of this realization were mind-blowing. I see all great works, including the great scientific discoveries and new inventions, as a manifestation of God's unceasing creation in the vast universe. He creates through us, since we were made in God's own image. God's creation is unceasing in the vast universe.

My theological thinking and intellectual growth were further enhanced when we discussed contemporary theological topics such as "Man come of age" and "God is dead!" As I reflect on those topics, I am ever grateful to God for having made us in his own image. Through us, God continues to do great works (John 14:12): "Very truly, I tell you, the one who believes in me will also do the works that I do and, in fact, will do greater works than these, because I am going to the Father" so when I think about "Man come of age" I envisage the mature human being who is free to explore his vast potential.

Furthermore, I found Bishop A. T. Robinson of Woolwich's pronouncement that Man had come of age intriguing. The human being is responsible for using the image of God to be a true coworker with God. In my estimation, "Man come of age" involves being aware of the indisputable need for justice, compassion, and forgiveness in order to live in love. Love should be the chief ingredient of "Man come of age." I found Dr. Joseph Fletcher's exposition of new Christian morality in "Situational Ethics" inadequate, as it was only based in law. The law is in itself insufficient without reference to justice, compassion, forgiveness, and love. Action in any contextual situation should be guided by love.

In Professor Day Williams's class we explored the "God is dead" theology. To some students this theology spelled blasphemy, but to some of us it had intrinsic pedagogical value. I personally valued it because, paradoxically, it illustrated that God cannot die as is exemplified in the resurrection of the Lord Jesus Christ. On the other hand, the "God is dead" debate made me realize that God does die to people who find God in "gaps." Such individuals only seek God when they are poor, sick, hungry, weak, and friendless. But when they are healthy and prosperous, they boast that it is their hard work and cleverness that enable them to attain their riches. There is a gap; God is left out. This, I have found, is the challenge of both rich people and rich nations.

The expression "God is dead" first appeared in Nietzsche's *The Gay Science* publication whereby "the madman" laments:

> God is dead. God remains dead. And we have killed him. How shall we comfort ourselves, the murderers of all murderers? What was holiest and mightiest of all that the world has yet owned has bled to death under our knives: who will wipe this blood off us?
>
> What water is there for us to clean ourselves? What festivals of atonement, what sacred games shall we have to invent? Is not the greatness of this deed too great for us? Must we ourselves not become gods simply to appear worthy of it?[2]

The fear and despair expressed by "the madman" were due to lack of appreciation that Jesus Christ's death on the cross was to atone for the sins of the world. His death was not an accident; it was preordained by God. In 1961, Gianni Vahanian published *Death of*

---

2. Friedrich Wilhem Nietzsche *The Gay Science* (New York Vintage Books, 1974), 181–82.

God in which he argued that modern secular culture had so lost all sense of the numinous that for all intents and purposes "God is dead" to the modern mind.

At UTS, I also studied the doctrine of the triune God[3] in depth. From this doctrine, I deduced that the death of Jesus Christ on the cross for the world was God's manifestation to humanity of his redemptive essence. It did not mean that when the Word became flesh by incarnation then God became minus the Word. No, God remained complete. Just as when one lights a candle from a mother candle's flames, the mother candle remains complete and burning. Thus God never dies and is not dying; he is the God of Man come of age and the God of babies. God is over all and in all. Some rich and powerful nations and people get so corrupted by power and wealth that they are even tempted to usurp the place of God. As such, they can potentially destroy the earth. The "God is dead" theology helped me realize that "God is being itself" as Paul Tillich put it. In the same way, we humans, having been made in the image of Being itself, shall never die. We are eternal.

At UTS I learned that a fully developed human being will be interested not only in his own selfish interests but also the interests of others. A mature human being is concerned about mother earth, which is now being depleted. In the twenty-first century, nations and societies are capable of producing enough to feed, clothe, and shelter all human beings, if only we can control the selfish side of our nature. I dreamt of a world where unemployment and under-employment would be eliminated, enabling every person to contribute according to his/her talent. The needs of the young, the aged, and the sick would be universally cared for. This utopian world is possible only if we remember that we are alive for God and for one another. We are God's stewards on the earth and beyond. It is our responsibility to preserve, conserve, and utilize our environment and resources to make life prosperous for everyone.

---

3. God the Father, the Son, and the Holy Spirit.

Unemployment is a colossal problem worldwide largely due to greed and corruption of the so-called "Man come of age." We cannot fully claim to "come of age" until we are aware of God's image in us. It is time we woke up and realized our obligations to love and serve God in one another.

In the course of my studies at Union, the works of the great theologian Anselm of Canterbury, whose motto was "faith seeking understanding," greatly shaped my thinking. Anselm argued that faith and reason go hand-in-hand. It should, however, be emphasized that faith precedes theology. We theologize on faith, but faith is not grounded in philosophy. Reason is used to understand faith. This knowledge has been the bedrock on which I base my work even when society attempts to discourage me. As I read the Holy Scriptures and listen to various religious discourses, I seek God's guidance and revelation (John 16:13) to enable me to employ reason to understand and act according to God's will. This foundation that I received at UTS has been the cornerstone of my ministry.

At UTS, I also studied "Christ and Culture" as expounded by H. Richard Niebuhr. Niebuhr argued that Christ transcended culture. Christ is simultaneously of culture and above culture; Christ transforms culture.

This understanding of Christ and culture has enabled and helped me enormously to face impediments, whether in African or other cultural settings. The question I always ask myself is: "What would Christ say about this cultural practice?" I believe that Christ is the litmus test of all cultural norms. This approach to culture has enabled me to be flexible. Because culture is not static, I readily accept positive changes that enhance my ethnic Buganda tradition. It is not enough to say "that is my culture," just as it is not enough to just say "that is my faith." I believe that is what Peter advised his readers to do:

> Be ready to make your defense to anyone who demands from you an account of the hope that is in you. (1 Pet. 3:15)

The Church of Epiphany in New York: The Foundation of My Ministry

As I prepared for ordination to the priesthood, the Rev. McCandless, with whom I worked as deacon, took me under his tutelage. The Rt. Rev. Dr. Leslie Brown, my bishop in Uganda, had requested him to prepare me for ordination. Dr. McCandless wholeheartedly accepted the bishop's request. He prepared me well, sharing with me his wisdom and his insights into the intricacies of being a priest. On December 19, 1964, Bishop Horace Donegan of the Diocese of New York ordained me as a priest at the Cathedral of St. John the Divine. Subsequently, I was licensed to work as a priest in the city of New York.

After my ordination, the Rev. McCandless linked me with the James Ewing Cancer Hospital (now Sloan Kettering Cancer Center), where I served as a chaplain. I worked at the hospital for two years alongside Rev. Sibly, who was a perpetual deacon there. Deaconess Sibly was a kind and social person. She taught me how to communicate with patients; among the important lessons she taught me was that the last sense to die in a patient is hearing. Even when a patient is unable to speak, the sense of hearing is often intact. Consequently, it is advisable to continue speaking loving words to patients until their last breaths.

A particularly memorable experience at the James Ewing Cancer Hospital involved a terminally ill lady, ravaged by cancer. She was in great pain, but she assured me that she was at peace because she knew that she was going to be with the Lord Jesus Christ. I was struck by her faith that rendered her placid in the face of death.

On May 2, 1966, our son, Joseph, was born at Woman's Hospital in New York City. That same year, I received my bachelor of divinity degree (now master of divinity) at UTS, and started studying for the master of sacred theology degree, which I received in 1967.

2

Returning to Uganda

IN AUGUST 1967, MARY, BABY JOSEPH, and I returned to Uganda via London, Paris, and Rome. In London we stayed at the home of the Rev. Eric Hutchison and his wife, Elspeth.

The cleanliness of Paris and its underground metro trains impressed us. Mary and I took turns exploring Paris, so that one of us could stay behind to take care of Joseph. I went first, but I could not find my way back to our hotel. Everything looked the same! I tried asking for directions but to no avail. Most people seemed to ignore me, as I could not speak French. Eventually some young people who spoke English directed me back to the hotel.

On my return, Mary, too, went out for a leisurely walk. Alas, she also got lost. I waited until dark. There was no sign of Mary. What would I tell my father-in-law, Mr. Eriyasafu Kyebakola, if I returned without Mary? Rather than return to Uganda without Mary, it would be better to immigrate to Europe, I told myself.

To baby Joseph's and my relief, Mary eventually returned. It was a fantastic reunion.

In Rome we visited St. Peter's Basilica and the Vatican. It was awe-inspiring to see the burial places of some of the forefathers of the church. We found the Italians friendly. Some of them told us that they had been contractors on road projects in Uganda. We were amused when they served us beer instead of water in a restaurant. After Rome we returned to Uganda. On my arrival in Uganda, I temporarily resumed work at my former church in Ntinda.

At the beginning of 1968, I was appointed vicar of Namirembe Cathedral, under the dean, the Very Rev. Yokana Mukasa.[1] Dean Mukasa guided me well, and granted me great freedom in practicing ministry. I learned a great deal as I handled various pastoral concerns at the cosmopolitan cathedral. One day, a woman came to the church seeking a divorce. I informed her that the church did not permit divorce. I advised her to reconcile with her husband. Her response was eye-opening: she blatantly told me that it was not the church that had made her fall in love with her husband in the first place. Likewise, the church could not reverse the loathing she now felt for him. This encounter was the catalyst of my interest to study marriage and divorce within the context of the ministry.[2] With the benefit of further study and experience as a married man myself, I eventually understood her position. It became clear that marriage is like a plant that needs tender nurturing all the time. Without those elements it withers and dies.

At the beginning of 1969, I was appointed a full-time lecturer at Bishop Tucker Theological College at Mukono. The rigorous studies at Union Theological Seminary had prepared me well to teach theology. At Bishop Tucker College, I taught three courses: "Work and Mission of the Church in the World," "African Traditional Religions," and "Systematic Theology."

In the "Work and Mission of the Church in the World" course, we discussed the then prevailing East African political treatises: "The Common Man's Charter in Uganda" and the Ujamaa villages in Tanzania. Beyond their economic shortfalls, these socialist experiments were seemingly well-meaning but were spoiled by careless and inhumane implementation. In the Christian context, the most damning shortcoming of these ideologies was the lack of

---

1. Rev. Yokana Mukasa later became the first bishop of Mityana Diocese, in 1976.

2. Much later in 1983, my doctor of ministry dissertation focused on marriage. It was titled: *Polygamy, Monogamy and Divorce: A Biblical, Historical, and African Perspective.*

respect for human rights and dignity. We also discussed the need for the church to understand and express its views on various government policies as they affect the human race. However, I told my students that while the church is in the world, she is not of the world. I used an analogy of a boat and the sea. The boat can be on the sea, but the sea cannot be on the boat, lest it sinks. Likewise, it would be catastrophic for the world to be in the church.

The "Common Man's Charter" was a document that President Milton Obote submitted to the ruling Ugandan People's Congress Party in 1969 at an emergency meeting called to restore confidence in the government following the tumultuous events that I discuss later. The document outlined his "move-to-the-left" policy.[3]

The "move-to-the left" was essentially an attempt to implement socialism in Uganda and to consolidate the president's power following his abolition of the monarchies of Buganda, Bunyoro, Ankole, and Busoga. On May 1, 1970, Obote outlined his Nakivubo Pronouncement,[4] which was designed to entrench his "move-to-the left" policy. The pronouncement declared that, with immediate effect, the government was to take a 60 percent stake (up from 51 percent) in over eighty corporations, including all banks, insurance companies, manufacturing and mining industries, plantations, oil companies, and transport entities. In addition, the policy imposed a government monopoly over import-export markets, with the exception of oil. Nevertheless, the policy was doomed because there were hardly any genuine socialists in Uganda, let alone ones with administrative ability.

In January 1971, when Idi Amin overthrew Obote in the military coup, the "move-to-the-left" policy was discontinued. On May 1, 1971, the incoming minister of finance declared that the

---

3. Dr. A. Milton Obote, "The Common Man's Charter" (Entebbe, Uganda: Government Printer, 1970).

4. Jesse Russel and Ronald Cohn, "Nakivubo Pronouncement" (Miami: Books on Demand, 2015).

new regime would choose elements of either socialism or capital-ism that were relative to Uganda's needs. Hence four banks, four insurance companies, two locally owned sugar companies, and the East African Steel Corporation, in which the government retained 49 percent stake, remained close to government control; all other firms would be completely private.

In the "Work and Mission of the Church in the World" class, we also discussed Tanzania's Ujamaa village socialist experiment. In the 1960s when many African countries gained independence, "African Socialism" was the popular catchword that captured the imagination of leaders such as Julius Nyerere of Tanzania, Ken-neth Kaunda of Zambia, and Milton Obote of Uganda. It envi-sioned universal prosperity for all citizens. In reality, while it was not complete communism as in China, it was very close to it. In 1965, Nyerere, the first elected president of postindependence Tanganyika declared a one-party state. He embarked on a policy of "African Socialism" which culminated in the 1967 Arusha Declara-tion,[5] which set the principles of "Ujamaa": collective production, equal opportunity, and above all, self-reliance. Social and economic development would be achieved through newly created "Ujamaa villages" to which the government relocated farmers to areas des-ignated for specific types of production. More than 8,000 such villages were created by the mid-1970s, but traditional resistance and a difficult economic environment led to the breakdown of this idealistic social program.

In the 1970s, I visited some Tanzanian villages bordering the fringes of my diocese. I was told that people were arbitrarily rounded up at night and forced to settle in far-off Ujamaa villages. This villagization policy caused resentment because not only did it dislocate people, but it also eliminated ancient traditional leader-ship structures.

---

5. Jannik Boesen, Birgt Storgard Madsen, Moody Tony, *Ujamaa—Socialism from Above* (Uppsala: Scandinavian Istitute of African Studeis, 1977).

In the "African Traditional Religions" course, we read the books by Professors John Mbiti and Bolaji Idowu. Their works helped me to relate Christ with culture. They also illustrated the fact that in traditional religions there are some aspects that can fulfill and even transform, yet there are others that cannot be reconciled with Christ, such as the subordination of women, discrimination, and human sacrifice.

One day, I ventured out on a field trip with my students in the class. One of the students, who knew a local traditional diviner, persuaded the diviner to let us visit his shrine. It was then that I realized that diviners had vestiges of power and could seemingly perform miracles. We saw an old woman, allegedly possessed by a local spirit "Kisekuzo," hit herself hard several times with a big club without getting hurt. The diviner then walked on red-hot burning charcoal while licking a red-hot knife's blade. We wondered whether it was simply magic or a case of the devil exhibiting his powers. After showing off, the diviner attempted to test our faith in the power of the Almighty God in whom we trust. As we left, he declared that the shrine's resident spiritual power had chosen the most beautiful girl among the students to remain behind. As the girl trembled with fear, I raised my voice and said: *"Christ is above the powers of Satan. Your request is impossible. The girl will not stay behind!"* The diviner was dumbfounded; we left without hindrance.

The experience of teaching in the theological college opened my eyes to some of the many problems that the church encounters in its ministry. Many people live in fear. And, like the diviner, the church sometimes uses intimidation to coerce people into certain positions. Nevertheless, God's people should stand their ground in the knowledge that God loves them. He is the Lord over even the evil spirits. As followers of Christ, we should be brave to rebuke the devil in Jesus's name.

In 1973, I was hired by the Uganda Bible Society to help translate the Bible into Luganda. I relinquished teaching at Bishop Tucker Theological College, where I had taught for four years.

The translation was an ecumenical Christian project that involved Roman Catholics, Greek Orthodox, Seventh Day Adventists (SDA), and Anglicans. The Rev. Fr. Dr. Francis Mbaziira and I were the two lead, full-time translators entrusted with the task; we were ably assisted by a small team that perused our translation section by section.

As we translated the New Testament, I realized that my studies of New Testament Greek at Buwalasi Theological College and at Union Theological Seminary had prepared me well for the task. My fellow translator, Dr. Mbaziira, was also well-versed in the New Testament Greek.

I left the Bible Society after one year, upon being elected bishop. Fortunately, Dr. Mbaziira saw the translation to completion. Our translation is still in use in Uganda's churches today.

Becoming a Bishop

In October 1973, trusted friends within the church informed me that I had been nominated to become the new bishop of West Buganda Diocese. I didn't think the nomination was serious. Within a month of hearing this news, the House of Bishops met at Bishop Tucker Theological College. Among the topics the bishops discussed was the election of a new bishop of West Buganda Diocese. Following the meeting, the Most Rev. Eric Sabiti, then archbishop of the Anglican Church of Uganda, Rwanda, and Boga-Zaire, summoned me to his office where he asked me whether I would accept if I were elected bishop. I was astonished and speechless for a moment. When I finally spoke, I told him that I could not answer immediately; I wanted to consult my wife first.

As I pondered my predicament, the archbishop looked at me and read John 21:18: "Very truly, I tell you, when you were younger, you used to fasten your own belt and to go wherever you wished. But when you grow old, you will stretch out your hands, and someone else will fasten a belt around you and take you where you do not wish to go." Those words were enough. I told the archbishop, "Here I am, I am ready to go wherever the Lord sends me." He responded, "You have been elected bishop in the Church of God, and are to be enthroned bishop of West Buganda."

I was overwhelmed with joy and trepidation. I rushed home to tell my wife. Mary and I thanked God for choosing me to feed his sheep, even though deep in my heart I felt that I was a bit too young and inexperienced for the responsibility that such a post entailed. I was not yet forty-two, but I was determined to obey God's bidding.

After my election, the church arranged for me to go to the United Kingdom to meditate and reflect in preparation for my duties as bishop. In December 1973, I flew to the UK. While there, I resided with my former bishop, the Rt. Rev. Dr. Leslie Brown, who was now the bishop of Ipswich. The bishop was a wise and humble man fully dedicated to God's service. His parishioners loved and respected him. He had neither servants nor children at home. He and his wife lived alone in the bishop's mansion. He confided in me that it was a challenge for them to maintain the residence at their relatively advanced age.

During my sojourn in England, I also relished visiting the Rev. Eric Hutchison, my mentor and former teacher, who was then living in Cambridge. He was busy counseling and applying his long-time interest in the prescriptions of the famous Swiss psychoanalyst, Carl Gustav Jung, whom he occasionally quoted while teaching at Buwalasi.

Toward the end of my forty-day stay in England, I visited Brighton, one of the United Kingdom's most beautiful cities. While there, I stayed with three old friends of West Buganda Diocese: Miss Winfred Milnes-Walker and her two younger sisters. The trio cared for me like a beloved brother in Christ Jesus. Miss Winfred Milness-Walker, who had worked for the Mother's Union of West Buganda Diocese, warned me about the danger of contracting malaria, particularly in Rakai, an area of the diocese for which she had great love. She recommended the use of a mosquito net as a precaution.

On my return to Uganda, in January 1974, Mary and I were enrolled in counseling sessions, in preparation for my service as bishop. The Rt. Rev. Dr. Dunstan Nsubuga of Namirembe Diocese, whom I regarded as a model bishop, coached me thoroughly and effectively. He taught me that a bishop is father of all people, Christians and non-Christians. He is a man of God, who welcomes everybody. He should be patient and should listen to all who come to him. The bishop should not only bear his own burdens, but bear the burdens of others as well. A bishop partakes in many feasts, but he should be aware of the pitfalls of overfeasting. Mary, my wife, would be my first assistant. She would, among other things, ensure that I eat and dress well in order to effectively serve God's flock. In the face of the burdens and challenges that come with the office, Mary and I would be responsible for each other's physical, mental, and spiritual well-being.

Being consecrated bishop was a special bestowment of grace from the benevolent Giver. I felt so humbled to be called to serve as bishop in the Church of God. I understood that I was called to

Photograph taken at Namirembe Cathedral after my consecration.

serve not because of my holiness, but rather because of the precious blood of the Lamb, the Son of God, that was shed for me. I could be bold to serve in his kingdom without fear, for he crucified all my sins on the cross.

On January 27, 1974, I was enthroned as the third bishop of West Buganda Diocese by the archbishop, the Most Rev. Eric Sabiti. The Anglican bishops of the Church Province of Uganda, Rwanda, and Boga-Zaire assisted and the primate of the Anglican Church of Canada preached. Mary was by my side, and our young children sat at the front of the church. Among the many relatives and friends present were my mother; my aunt, Yudesi Nanyonga; and my uncle, Douglas Kyeyune, and his wife, Maama Miriam Kyeyune.

The function took place at St. Paul's Cathedral, Kako, the headquarters of the diocese. In my sermon, I emphasized the need to be reconciled to God and to one another (2 Cor. 5:18–6:2):

> All this is from God, who reconciled us to himself through Christ, and has given us the ministry of reconciliation; that is, in Christ God was reconciling the world to himself, not counting their trespasses against them, and entrusting the message of reconciliation to us. So we are ambassadors for Christ, since God is making his appeal through us; we entreat you on behalf of Christ, be reconciled to God. For our sake he made him to be sin who knew no sin, so that in him we might become the righteousness of God. As we work together with him, we urge you also not to accept the grace of God in vain. For he says, "At an acceptable time I have listened to you, and on a day of salvation I have helped you." See, now is the acceptable time; see, now is the day of salvation!

Indeed, reconciliation would become the cornerstone of my service in West Buganda Diocese. It still is today as I minister to the marginalized, the oppressed, and the ostracized. God revealed to me the need to foster reconciliation in West Buganda Diocese and elsewhere.

At the time of my enthronement in 1974, West Buganda Diocese was geographically very large. In the northwest, it bordered Bunyoro, by the River Kafu; in the west, along the Mubende-Fort Portal Highway, it bordered Toro Kingdom; in the southwest, along the Masaka-Mbarara Highway, it bordered Ankole; and directly south, along the Masaka-Mutukula Road, it bordered Tanzania. Nangoma, on Lake Victoria's shoreline, which could conceivably be part of Bukoba District in Tanzania, was also part of my diocese. Sometimes, I would go on pastoral visits to Nangoma by car via Bukoba. Most times, however, I took a shorter route by canoe on vast Lake Victoria. On one memorable occasion, a small canoe, which was carrying me and a few others, almost capsized. The Rev. Erasmus Nsamba, a young priest who had accompanied me, got so frightened that he vowed that he would never again travel by boat to Nangoma!

My largely rural diocese was mostly traversed by unpaved roads. During the dry season, my driver, Mr. Bbasi, and I would often reach our destination covered in brown, white, or red dust. And during the rainy season the roads sometimes became so slippery that we got stuck in the mud. One day, as we drove in the dark at night on our way to Kakabagyo Parish via Lyantonde, we encountered a flooded road, surrounded by swamps. Given the circumstances, including poor visibility, we decided it was not wise to try to navigate through the waters. We improvised, cutting some of the nearby banana plantation's trees in a bid to create a bypass path to a safer, unflooded portion of the road. As we hurriedly cut the plantation's trees, we feared that the owners would see us and attack us with machetes and spears. But, by the grace of God, they did not. They were probably afraid to attack the intrepid strangers.[6] Nonetheless, we took the trouble to explain our situation to them and to apologize; they graciously let us proceed to our destination without any hindrance.

---

6. In some of these parts, cars were scarce. The few cars that traversed through often belonged to powerful government authorities, who could be ruthless if provoked.

The Anglicans in West Buganda Diocese were very generous. They endeavored to ensure that I had the means to adequately serve the diocese in the dignity befitting the office.[7] They were devout and loyal to the church. During the hard times of Idi Amin, the church sustained their faith, and was the only independent institution that voiced their concerns. It offered them spiritual refuge and comfort.

The parishes looked forward to my annual confirmation visits. On arrival in the vicinity of a parish, I would find them lined up along the roads which they had decorated with banana trees and flowers, singing welcome songs, celebrating, and dancing. Church services were invariably followed by communal feasts. And as a gesture of their appreciation and love, parishioners often gave me gifts, including fine china, food, and even live animals: goats, cows, sheep, and chicken for rearing![8]

Due to long distances in the vast diocese, I occasionally spent nights in local members' homes, irrespective of the conditions of their dwellings. On one of my overnight visits in Rakai, I was bitten by a snake while in bed sleeping. The hosts immediately gave me first aid. I was greatly concerned about the people whom I was to confirm there. As I received treatment, I directed the priests to quickly summon the confirmation candidates to the house so that I could confirm them. After the confirmations, I was taken to Dr. Byansi's clinic in Masaka town. The doctor treated me until all snake-bite symptoms dissipated.

It was at times difficult to actualize money projected in the diocesan budget. At such times keeping up the diocesan staff's morale was a challenge. To make up for the shortfalls, we would borrow money from the diocese's bank. But giving improved as we taught Christians that they were God's stewards; they should support his service, for it is more blessed to give than to receive (Acts 20:35).

---

7. This was done by buying me a brand new Mercedes Benz.

8. It is impolite and in fact offensive in our culture to refuse gifts.

Due to their greater capacity to give, a few well-to-do Christians in my diocese sought to have the last word on everything; they felt that the diocese should be run at their behest and bidding. I reminded them over and over again that the Church is the body of Christ, whose will we must all seek.

Reconciliation in West Buganda Diocese

Christians in the diocese were worryingly divided. The first bishop of the diocese, the Rt. Rev. Festo Lutaya, had sought to transfer the headquarters of the diocese from Kako, in Masaka District, to Mityana, in Mubende District. But while Mityana had more Anglicans than Masaka, which was predominantly Catholic, it did not yet possess sufficient facilities to accommodate diocesan headquarters.

In the meantime, Bishop Lutaya decided to reside at both Kako and Mityana. Prominent Christians in Masaka led by Mr. Yokana Mukasa, a wealthy farmer and landowner, opposed his position. And while the diocesan council agreed with the bishop, Archbishop Leslie Brown disagreed with him. The archbishop replaced Bishop Lutaya with Bishop Stephen Tomusange, who firmly reestablished the diocese's headquarters at Kako. The dethroned bishop refused to acknowledge the ruling; instead he chose to establish headquarters at Mityana. This state of affairs led to the formation of two competing factions within the diocese.

Even though some Christians in Mityana sympathized with Bishop Festo Lutaya, the church no longer recognized him as having jurisdiction over any part of the diocese. The Christians and the few priests who supported him chose to boycott church services. Bishop Lutaya stayed put in his residence. But per church edict, officials in the diocese could no longer visit with him, and were in fact urged to disown him. The clergy who were once closest to him became distant strangers. Most of his contemporaries would not even afford him transport in their cars. He became an isolated, lonely old man. This was, I decided, an unacceptable scandal within the Church of God.

That was the unhealthy state of affairs in the diocese at the time I was enthroned as its bishop in1974.

Much of this information was related to me by my predecessor's driver, Mr. Paulo Bbasi. Mr. Bbasi also served as my driver for the entire twenty-four years that I was diocesan bishop of West Buganda. Older than me, Mr. Bbasi was a quiet, intelligent, and wise man. He knew the diocese and its people quite well. While driving through the vast diocese, he would share a lot of pertinent information with me.[9] Through his stories, I understood the genesis of the problems in the diocese.

By the end of 1974, I had already canvassed the cooperation and support of some key Christians, such as Mr. Douglas Kasolo and the Rev. Canon Kezekiya Kalule, in a bid to resolve the crisis that had gripped the diocese. I also got great assistance from former Katikkiro (prime minister) of Buganda, the Hon. Paulo Kavuma. I worked hard to convince Bishop Festo Lutaya that reconciliation was possible, and to show the clergy that the church is a place of peace, love, and forgiveness.

Archdeacon Ezra Kamya of Mityana, who had been charged with implementing church orders to deprive Bishop Lutaya of his authority, ultimately came on board. It helped that Archbishop Leslie Brown, who had sacked Bishop Lutaya, had retired and returned to England. Archbishop Eric Sabiti, who had succeeded him, had also retired. The new archbishop, the Most Rev. Janani Luwum, embraced my efforts to reconcile the diocese with his unreserved blessing and support. Bishop Festo Lutaya and I agreed to pray that God would enable us to attain the reconciliation that we sought.

---

9. I thank God that I was invited and allowed to officiate at his funeral after my retirement, even though the church had by then already ostracized me due to my refusal to stop ministering to lesbian, gay, bisexual, and transgender (LGBT) persons.

By the grace of God, Bishop Festo Lutaya eventually agreed to vacate his headquarters (the bishop's residence) at Mityana; he retired honorably to his home at Busega, near Kampala. Much of the credit is due to Mr. Douglas Kasolo, a go-between and negotiator, who did a terrific job. I am also very grateful to Bishop Lutaya, whose humility and prayers enabled us to achieve reconciliation. Above all, I thank God for answering our prayers.

To commemorate the achievement, we arranged a church service at the Mityana Archdeaconry's Principal Church where Bishop Lutaya had placed his headquarters. The archbishop of Uganda, His Grace, the Most Rev. Janani Luwum, presided over the service. When it was Bishop Festo Lutaya's turn to speak, he rather cryptically said, "It is not possible to express my experience in the abode of the dead, the Hades."

Bishop Lutaya was once again free to preach and to officiate at any occasion as bishop, when invited. In 1975, Mary and I invited

The photograph was taken showing L–R; Bishop Steven Tomusange and his wife; Bishop Lutaya and his wife; Bishop Christopher Senyonjo and his wife; and Rev. Canon Esau Sendiwala of Kako Cathedral before the dinner at Kako residence.

Bishop Lutaya and his wife, as well as my immediate predecessor, Bishop Stephen Tomusange and his wife, to a dinner at the West Buganda Diocese bishop's residence at Kako. Many guests graced this joyful occasion.

The Formation of Mityana Diocese

The formation of Mityana Diocese became possible after reconciliation was achieved. Masaka Christians conceded to Bishop Lutaya's long-held view that since Kako and Mityana were far apart, there was need for a diocese at Mityana to serve the northwestern sections of the vast diocese. In 1976, the West Buganda Diocesan Synod passed a resolution to carve "Singo-Buwekula" Diocese from West Buganda. The proposed diocese was later renamed Mityana Diocese by its first synod. Mr. Kalanzi and the Hon. Paulo Kavuma mobilized the resources necessary to ensure the viability of the new diocese. The Very Rev. Yokana Mukasa, dean of Namirembe Diocese, was elected to serve as the inaugural bishop of Mityana Diocese. The archbishop, the Most Rev. Janani Luwum, consecrated and enthroned the Mukasa bishop at a joyous occasion in Mityana.

In 1994, Central Buganda Diocese was carved from my West Buganda Diocese upon request. My assistant, the Rt. Rev. Dr. George Sinabulya, was enthroned first bishop of the new diocese, with its headquarters at Kasaka. This growth of the church was only possible through the spirit of reconciliation.

Building the New Cathedral at Kako

On becoming bishop of West Buganda Diocese, I embraced the task of building the new cathedral that my predecessor Bishop Stephen Tomusange had envisioned. Architect Kawesa drew up the master plan of the new cathedral and before he retired, Bishop Tomusange dug the foundation of the new church. In 1974, I officially dedicated the construction of the new cathedral with a foundation stone.

My team and I designed a plan to fundraise and mobilize Christians for the building effort.[10] On all my confirmation parish visits, I collected contributions toward the construction of the new cathedral. I am grateful to His Eminence Emmanuel Cardinal Nsubuga, then premier of the Catholic Church in Uganda, for his contribution toward the new Anglican cathedral. He graced us with his presence as chief guest at a fundraising function held at Rubaga Conference Centre where we collected millions of shillings for the construction effort.

By the end of 1978, we had purchased the majority of the building materials, but in 1979, during the ensuing war that ousted Idi Amin, all the materials, including roofing beams worth 30 million shillings (which was a lot of money then), were stolen. It was a huge setback. Nonetheless, we did not lose heart. We continued to mobilize resources, and by the time I retired in 1998, the cathedral had reached roofing stage.

On August 30, 2009, my successor, the Rt. Rev. Dr. Kefa Ssemakula Kamya officially opened the new cathedral. I felt honored when he graciously invited me as a guest. I am very grateful to him for completing the magnificent cathedral. Prominently erected on the cathedral are three crosses donated by Mr. Asafu Mukalazi. The middle cross represents the cross on which Jesus was crucified; the other two crosses represent the crosses of the two thieves that were crucified along with our Lord.

Managing Diocesan Affairs

The duties of a bishop are quite extensive. The bishop is not only the chief pastor and custodian of the faith, he is also the chief administrator, chief executive, and chairman of the boards of

---

10. Key building team members included: Mr. Asafu Mukalazi—treasurer of the Cathedral Fund; The Rev. Canon Erisa Wamala, supervisor and coordinator of the building effort; and Mr. Kakuru, a skillful builder from Ankole.

various church enterprises. In addition, he is chief guardian of the church's land and properties. In this regard, I found that delegating responsibilities relieved me of undue stress. Experience taught me, however, that one needs to delegate carefully. Some of the senior clergy, such as the archdeacons and the canons, attempted to assume responsibilities that could have curtailed the smooth running of the diocese. In regards to many tasks, they would say, "Leave that to me," "I will see to it." In Luganda, such persons were nicknamed "Kindekere" (Leave-it-to-mes). Thus, I tried to avoid delegating too many responsibilities to any single person.

The senior clergy were my chief advisors on diocesan affairs, including the transfer of priests among parishes. Many priests dreaded the transfers. Some even attempted to ingratiate themselves with my wife by increasing the frequency of their visits to our home in the hope that she would influence me on their behalf.

Parish priests were generally hard working and played a key role in mobilizing and engaging Christians. And, as their bishop, they endeavored to please me. On my part, since the church's pension offering was rather meager, I often advised them to plan early for retirement. I also urged them to identify supplementary sources of long-term income.

In running the diocese, I employed a business team to help me manage a variety of income-generating diocesan projects. Two of these projects, Bulayi Coffee and Tea Farm and the Mawogola Cattle Ranch, were quite lucrative. Such projects generated funds for workers' salaries and for charitable community services. Without qualified accountants, managers, and a governing board, it would have been impossible for me to supervise and ensure the success of such projects. The governing board reported to the diocesan council, which I chaired.

A team of responsible and efficient secretaries also assisted me. In addition, Mary was an indispensable assistant. I referred to her as my bishop. She gave me frank counsel. She also graciously welcomed and entertained multitudes of visitors to our home. They came at all times, often without prior notice, as telephone service was almost nonexistent in rural Uganda.

The Mother's Union

Strong Christian families are essential to the vitality of the church. Mothers play the preeminent role in family strength and unity. Thus, as bishop, I worked closely with the Mother's Union.[11] My strong support of the Mother's Union was recognized throughout the province of the Church of Uganda. Consequently, in 1979, Mrs. Janet Wesonga from Mbale Diocese, Dr. Nsubuga from Busoga Diocese, and I represented the Church of Uganda at the Mother's Union conference in Australia. We visited Brisbane, Sydney, Melbourne, and Canberra, Australia's well-planned capital. We also toured the eastern coast of Australia. On drives through the Australian countryside, I saw impressive eucalyptus forests and banana plantations that reminded me of home. The magnificence of the Sydney Opera and the cleanliness of the cities left a lasting impression on me.

We also met the Aborigines, many of whom lived in rather impoverished settlements. Their situation reminded me of the need to employ God's love and reconciliation in the affairs of the state.

The Youth

In addition, to women's groups, I also worked with youth groups. My conviction is that young people need guidance, first and foremost from their homes. The church and school should play supplementary roles. In any community, parents, teachers, and religious institutions should embrace a symbiotic relationship in the raising of children. It is not right, for instance, for parents to leave the

---

11. My wife, Mary, also served with distinction as the president of West Buganda Diocese's Mother's Union.

responsibility of ensuring proper education and discipline of their children to teachers, nor is it right for teachers or the state to expect that all parents are equally capable of nurturing the intellectual and emotional growth of their children. Further, parents should involve the youth in church in order to ground them in spirituality and the moral teachings of the church, particularly regarding love, justice, equity, and honesty. These are the foundations of an ethical and peaceful society. On the youth's part, it is important that they seek the wisdom of their elders. The unprecedented amount of information that youth can now access via the Internet is no substitute to the wisdom that their parents and grandparents can confer on them by virtue of their vast experience.

My Service in West Buganda Diocese

I shall never forget the warm welcome that my family and I received in 1974 on arrival at Lwera, near Lukaya town, on our way to the headquarters of West Buganda Diocese at Kako. We were greatly entertained by a jubilant crowd singing and dancing as they welcomed us. Mrs. Janet Kaziringa was particularly memorable. She led a repetitive chant in Luganda: "Mundabiranga ddala" which loosely translates as: "Always remember me."

I thank God for keeping me healthy for the twenty-four years that I served in the diocese. Not once during that period was I admitted to a hospital. On reflection, I believe that my decision to prepare and distribute yearlong itineraries to parishes in advance contributed to my peace of mind. Of course, as the chief pastor in the diocese, I allowed for flexibility in the itinerary in case of emergencies and unforeseen events.

3

The Martyrdom of
Archbishop Janani Luwum

The Arrest of Archbishop Janani Luwum

Archbishop Eric Sabiti retired not long after my enthronement as
bishop of West Buganda. The Most Rev. Janani Luwum, then bishop
of northern Uganda, who had also been one of my teachers at
Buwalasi Theological College, succeeded Sabiti. Following further
theological studies in London, the Rev. Luwum had been promoted
to become principal of Buwalasi Theological College. In 1966, he
was appointed provincial secretary of the Church of Uganda. And
in 1969, he was enthroned as bishop of northern Uganda at a service that was attended by the prime minister, Milton Obote, and
the chief of staff of the army, General Idi Amin Dada. In 1971, Idi
Amin overthrew Obote in a coup d'état and instituted army rule.

In 1974 Bishop Janani Luwum was enthroned archbishop
of the Church of Uganda, Rwanda, Burundi, and Boga-Zaire. He
ascended to the office during a tumultuous period. Idi Amin's security agencies were running amok, arresting and killing innocent
civilians with seeming impunity. The archbishop spoke out against
the atrocities and personally went to the offices of the dictator's
notorious "State Research Bureau" to secure the release of prisoners. The archbishop firmly resolved that the church should not suc-
cumb to the "forces of darkness."

The archbishop also spoke out against Idi Amin's attempts
to convert Christians to Islam. When the West decided to isolate
Amin due to rampant human right abuses and arbitrary rule, Amin
turned to King Faisal of Saudi Arabia and to President Muammar

Gaddafi of Libya for financial and spiritual support. The two Arab leaders encouraged him to follow through with his plan to ensure that Uganda would become a Muslim state. On his visit to Uganda in 1973, President Gaddafi promised to provide Amin with the resources necessary to establish such a state.

At 1:30 a.m. on February 5, 1977, government soldiers invaded the archbishop's official residence. They marched the prelate at gunpoint around the residence's large compound ostensibly so that he could show them hidden weapons.[1] Finding no weapons, they left.

On February 8, 1977, the archbishop summoned the bishops to a meeting at Namirembe Guest House where he narrated the stunning events to us. In response, we wrote the following letter of concern to the president protesting against both the degrading treatment of the archbishop and the rampant violation of human rights:[2]

Your Excellency,

We, the Archbishop and the bishops of the province of Uganda, Rwanda, Burundi and Boga-Zaire, meeting at Namirembe on Tuesday, February 8, 1977, humbly beg to submit our most deeply felt concern for the church and welfare of the people whom we serve under your care.

In presenting this document, we are in no way questioning the right of the government in administering justice to search and arrest offenders. We believe that the government has established structures and procedures that give the citizens a sense of what to expect of their government.

These structures and procedures give the police, the intelligence and security forces a framework within which to work. When these procedures are followed in carrying out their day-to-day duties, this gives the ordinary citizen a sense of security.

---

1. We later learned that the home of Bishop Yona Okoth in Tororo had also been invaded and searched on the same night.

2. The New Vision Printing and Publishing Co. Ltd.

But when the police and security officers deviate from these established structures and procedures in carrying out their day-to-day duties, citizens become insecure, afraid and disturbed. They begin to distrust these officers.

We are deeply disturbed to learn of the incident, which occurred at the Archbishop's official residence in the early hours of Saturday morning, February 5, 1977. In the history of our country, such an incident with the church has never before occurred.

Security officers broke through the fence and forced their way into the Archbishop's compound. They used a man they had arrested and tortured as a decoy to entice the Archbishop to open his door to help a man seemingly in distress.

Using a man under duress and torture as a source of information can lead to unnecessary suffering of innocent individuals.

The Archbishop opened his door. At that point, armed men who had been hiding sprung to attack and cocked their rifles, demanding "arms."

When the Archbishop asked, "[W]hat arms?" the answer was a muzzle of a rifle pressed against his stomach and immediately he was pushed forcefully into his house with the demand, "Archbishop, show us the arms, run into the bedroom."

First, we want to register our shock and protest at this kind of treatment to the top leader of the Church of Uganda, Rwanda, Burundi and Boga-Zaire. Then we shall draw out the implications of this incident for the rest of the bishops and all the Christians of the Church of Uganda.

Your Excellency, you have said publicly on many occasions that religious leaders have a special place in this country and that you treat them with respect for what they stand for and represent, you have on many occasions publicly demonstrated this and we are grateful. But what happened to the Archbishop in his house on the morning we have referred to is a direct contradiction to what you yourself, Your Excellency, have said in public and to the established structures and procedures in dealing with security matters.

This is why we are very disturbed and with us, the whole of the Church of Uganda.

We feel that if it is necessary to search the Archbishop's house, he should have been approached in broad daylight by responsible senior officers, fully identified in conformity with his position in society. But to search him and his house at gunpoint in the night leaves us without words. Now that the security of the Archbishop is at stake, the security of the bishops is more in jeopardy. Indeed, we have a case in point.

The night following the raid on the Archbishop's house, one of us, the Bishop of Bukedi, was searched and arrested. It was only when nothing could be found at his personal and official residences that he was later released on Sunday morning. This left the people in his diocese wondering and the wondering is spreading quickly. The Christians are asking: If this is happening to our bishops, then where are we?

The gun whose muzzle has been pressed against the Archbishop's stomach, the gun which has been used to search the Bishop of Bukedi's house, is the gun which is being pointed at every Christian in the Church.

The security of the ordinary people has been in jeopardy for quite a long time. It may be that what has happened to the Archbishop and the Bishop of Bukedi is a climax of what is consistently happening to our Christians.

We have buried many who have died as a result of being shot and there are many more whose bodies have not been found, yet their disappearance is connected with the activities of some members of security forces.

Your Excellency, if it is required, we can give concrete evidence of what is happening because widows and orphans are members of the church.

Furthermore, we are saddened by forces that are increasingly setting Ugandans one against another. While it is common in Uganda for members of one family to be members of different religious organizations, there is an increasing feeling that one particular religious organization is being favoured more than any other. So much so that, in some parts of Uganda, members of Islam, who are in leading positions, are using these positions to coerce Christians into becoming Muslims.

Secondly, members of the security forces are sons of civilians and they have civilian brothers and sisters. When they begin to use the gun in their hand to destroy instead of protecting the civilians, then the relationship, mutual trust and respect are destroyed. Instead of that relationship you have suspicion, fear and hidden hatred. There is also a war against the educated, which is forcing many of our people to run away from this country in spite of what the country has paid to educate them. This brain drain of our country, the fear and the mistrust make development, progress and stability of our country almost impossible.

The gun which was meant to protect Uganda as a nation, the Ugandan as a citizen and his property is increasingly being used against Ugandans to take away their life and property. For instance, many cars almost daily are being taken at gunpoint and their owners killed. And most of the culprits are never brought to justice. If required, we can enumerate many cases.

Too much power has been given to members of State Research Bureau, who arrest and kill at will innocent individuals. Therefore, that which meant to provide the Ugandan citizen with security is increasingly becoming the means of this insecurity.

We are also concerned about the developing gap between the leaders of the Christian churches, Archbishops in particular and Your Excellency. We had been assured by you of your availability to religious leaders whenever they had serious matters to discuss with you. You had even gone to the extent of giving His Grace, the Archbishop, the surest means of contacting you in this country wherever you may be. But a situation has developed now where you have become more and more inaccessible to the Archbishop and even when he tried to write, he has not received any reply.

This has brought a sad feeling of estrangement and alienation not only to the Archbishop and the bishops, but also it is reaching down to the ordinary citizens. While you, Your Excellency, have stated on the national radio that your government is not under any foreign influence and that your decisions are guided by your Defense Council and Cabinet, the general trend of things in Uganda has created a feeling that the affairs of our nation are being directed by outsiders, who do not have the welfare of this country and the values of the lives and properties of Ugandans at heart.

A situation like this breeds unnecessary misunderstandings and mistrust. Indeed, we were shocked to hear over the radio on Christmas Day, Your Excellency saying that some bishops had preached bloodshed. We waited anxiously to be called by Your Excellency to clarify on such a serious situation but all in vain. Your Excellency, we want to say here again that we are ready to come to you whenever there are serious matters that concern the Church and the nation. You have got only to call us. This used to be so, Your Excellency, when you freely moved among us and we freely came to you.

The Archbishop is not only the Archbishop of the Church of Uganda, but he is the Archbishop of the Church of Rwanda, Burundi and Boga-Zaire. So what happens to him here is also the concern of Christians in Rwanda, Burundi and Zaire. In fact, it goes further than that because he is the Archbishop of the Anglican Communion, which is a world-wide community, so are the bishops. An action such as this damages the good image of our nation. It also threatens our preparations for the Centenary celebrations.

Christians everywhere have become very cautious about taking part in the fundraising activities of the church for fear of being misrepresented and misinterpreted. The ban on sale of items donated for fundraising in aid of the church is a case in point. This too, could have [been] cleared if only Your Excellency had given the Archbishop the opportunity to brief you on the matter.

In addition to the concern of the Christians in the Anglican Communion, there is also the concern of the Christians of other denominations in Uganda and all over the world with whom we are in fellowship.

In conclusion, Your Excellency, we are grateful that you have given us this opportunity to express our grievances and concerns to you.

We all appended our names and signatures to the letter. The next day the archbishop delivered it to the office of the president.

Idi Amin's Response to the Bishops' Missive

When President Amin received the letter, he became extremely angry. He decided to stop the opposition by the church once and for all. He summoned the archbishop to meet him at the International Conference Centre in Kampala on February 16, 1977.

On the receipt of the summons, the archbishop invited the bishops to accompany him to the meeting. A few of us assembled at Namirembe Guest House on February 15, 1977, to prepare for the meeting with the president on the following day.

We spent the night at the guest house with the archbishop, for we were apprehensive that some misfortune could befall him if he spent the night at his official residence.

In the morning of February 16, 1977, before we set off for the encounter with the president, we prayed together and read a passage from Mark 4:35–41:

On the evening of that same day Jesus said to his disciples, "Let us go across to the other side of the lake." So they left the crowd; the disciples got into the boat in which Jesus was already sitting, and they took him with them. Other boats were there too. Suddenly a strong wind blew up, and the waves began to spill over into the boat, so that it was about to fill with water. Jesus was in the back of the boat, sleeping with his head on a pillow. The disciples woke him up and said, "Teacher, don't you care that we are about to die?"

Jesus stood up and commanded the wind, "Be quiet!" and he said to the waves, "Be still!" The wind died down, and there was a great calm. Then Jesus said to his disciples, "Why are you frightened? Have you still no faith?" But they were terribly afraid and said to one another, "Who is this man? Even the wind and the waves obey him!" (Good News Translation [GNT])

After prayer and the reading of the Scripture, we felt strengthened. Just as the disciples were urged to abandon fear and have faith in God, we set off believing that God was with us.

On February 16, 1977, six bishops: the Rt. Rev. Dunstan Nsubuga, the Rt. Rev. Silvanus Wani, the Rt. Rev. Festo Kivengere, the Rt. Rev. Yona Okoth, and I, along with a senior priest, the Rev. Canon Akisoferi Wesonga (then provincial secretary of the Church of Uganda) accompanied the archbishop to the meeting with the president at the International Conference Center.

The Scene at the International Conference Centre

We arrived at the International Conference Centre, the venue of our meeting with the president, by 9 o'clock that morning. As soon as we arrived, we realized that this was not going to be an ordinary meeting. There was a large crowd, among whom I noticed his Eminence Emmanuel Cardinal Nsubuga, dressed in a black suit instead of the usual cassock.

We were met by a rowdy and hostile contingent of soldiers in army combat uniform. Ominously, when Colonel Maliyamungu, their commander, asked them: "What do you want to do to these people?" they responded in unison, "Kill them, kill them, kill them!"

We were then paraded outside on the pavement. As secretary of the House of Bishops, I stood next to the archbishop and held his briefcase. We stood under the scorching sun for six hours, from 9 a.m. to 3 p.m. As the youngest of the eight clergy, I felt extremely sad for the Rt. Rev. Dunstan Nsubuga and the Rt. Rev. Silvanis Wani, the two elderly bishops among us. I worried about their capacity to bear standing in scorching heat for such a long time.

After some time, Colonel Maliyamungu read a lengthy document filled with serious allegations against the archbishop, including a plot to overthrow the government.[3] The commander pointed to a heap of weapons that he alleged were an exhibit of what church leaders were planning to do. But he did not say where the weapons were found. It was by the grace of God that none of us fainted or collapsed due to heat, exhaustion, or terror as we heard the accusations. It was neither our own wit nor our bravery that kept us in sound bodies and minds. While still in formation outside, we heard intermittent bursts of noise emanating from inside the International Conference Centre—the center's basement housed some of the regime's most notorious torture chambers.

At 3 p.m. we were led to a small room inside the building. We were virtual prisoners. Offered chairs, I sat next to the archbishop, as I was still holding his briefcase. We waited anxiously for what seemed like hours, under the careful guard of security agents, most of whom wore plain clothes. The room was stuffy and uncomfortable and we were thirsty. We asked for some water from girls in the room. The girls kindly brought us two glasses of water, which we communally shared.

At 5:30 p.m., we heard voices receding from the conference center. Five minutes later, a man in plain clothes entered the room. In an authoritative voice, he said, "You bishops should go now," but as the archbishop was getting up, the man told him, "The president wants you to sign something after which you will join the bishops outside." The archbishop asked me to hand him his briefcase. I did not imagine that would be the last time I saw him in this life.

Bishop Silvanus Wani tried to follow the archbishop as he was being led away, but commandos in army uniform pushed him away. It was then that it dawned on us that the archbishop had been arrested. We attempted to wait for him outside, but the soldiers furiously ordered us to leave the premises. As we left, we noted that one of us, Bishop Yona Okoth, had been singled out as one of the collaborators

---

3. Bishop Yona Okoth was also mentioned as a collaborator in the plot.

in a plot to overthrow the government. We feared for his safety, especially after we learned about the arrest of two other individuals who had been named in the alleged plot, Cabinet Ministers Erinayo Wilson Oryema and Charles Oboth Ofumbi. I advised Bishop Okoth to escape as soon as possible. He quickly made his way to exile; from then he referred to me as his Good Samaritan and friend.

The rest of us went to the archbishop's residence at Namirembe to try to comfort his wife, Mary. On seeing us without her husband, the archbishop's wife asked: "Where have you left my husband?" Touched by the entreaty, the archbishop's driver immediately drove back to the conference center to fetch the archbishop, but he was turned away at gunpoint.

The Martyrdom of Archbishop Janani Luwum

On the morning of February 17, 1977, a few of us went to the Church of Uganda Province's headquarters to consult with the provincial secretary, the Rev. Canon Akisoferi Wesonga. When I knocked on the door, Canon Wesonga opened it for us with tears running down his face. In a whisper, he told us that the archbishop was dead. We were shocked, shaken, and terrified. We also feared for our lives. As I hurried home, I bought a copy of *The Uganda Argus*, a daily government newspaper. The front page story quoted a government spokesman indicating that the archbishop and the two cabinet ministers had died in a car accident. I knew without a doubt that it was a pure lie.

Accounts of the Archbishop's Death

According to various intelligence accounts, Idi Amin asked the archbishop to sign a document implicating him and the church in a plot to overthrow the government. It is speculated that the document could have been used to justify banning both the Anglican and Catholic Churches in Uganda, paving the way to the dictator's dream of a Muslim state. When the archbishop refused to sign, he was beaten, kicked, and finally shot by Idi Amin himself as the archbishop prayed.[4]

Bishop Dunstan Nsubuga of Namirembe Diocese tried hard to claim the archbishop's body, but the president refused to release it. Instead, the authorities sent the body in a sealed casket under tight security to the archbishop's home village in Muchwini, Kitgum District. When the villagers opened the casket, they noticed that the body had several bullet wounds. The two cabinet ministers who had been implicated in the alleged plot were also killed with the archbishop. In his book, *A State of Blood,* Mr. Henry Kyemba, then a cabinet minister, stated that, "the bodies (of the Archbishop and the two ministers) were bullet-riddled. The Archbishop had been shot through the mouth and had at least three bullets in the chest."[5]

I concluded that Archbishop Luwum died a martyr's death. Indeed, he is now officially recognized by the global Anglican Church as one of the martyrs of the twentieth century. His statue was instated on the front west gate of Westminster Abbey in London and was officially unveiled in 1998. The Anglican Church commemorates his martyrdom on February 17th.

The Aftermath of the Archbishop's Death

I went home and shared with my wife what had happened. On reflection, Mary and I mutually agreed that it was dangerous for me to stay at the official bishop's residence. Other bishops likewise contemplated their situations. My brothers in Christ, the Rt. Rev. Yona Okoth, bishop of Bukedi; the Rt. Rev. Festo Kivengere, bishop of Kigezi; the Rt. Rev. Melkisedek Otim, bishop of Lango; and the Rt. Rev. Benon Ogwal, bishop of northern Uganda, went to exile abroad.

---

4. *http://allafrica.com/stories/200612180652.html.*

5. Henry Kyemba, *A State of Blood: The Inside Story of Idi Amin* (New York: Ace Books, 1977), 189.

I, on the other hand, sought internal refuge at my Uncle Potino Ganafa's home, far away in a remote part of Kiboga District. My uncle welcomed me and devised means to conceal me. I stayed at his home incognito. I blended into the home by wearing the Kanzu, a traditional Buganda tunic, but I largely stayed out of public view.

I kept my sanity by praying and reading every day. I believed that God was with me in my situation. I put all my trust in God. I was also greatly comforted by the solidarity expressed through many messages sent to me by my brothers and sisters in Christ. Many of them quoted Saint Paul's words in his letter to the Romans:

> We know that all things work together for good for those who love God, who are called according to his purpose. . . .
>
> What then are we to say about these things? If God is for us, who is against us? He who did not withhold his own Son, but gave him up for all of us, will he not with him also give us everything else? Who will bring any charge against God's elect? It is God who justifies. Who is to condemn? It is Christ Jesus, who died, yes, who was raised, who is at the right hand of God, who indeed intercedes for us. Who will separate us from the love of Christ? Will hardship, or distress, or persecution, or famine, or nakedness, or peril, or sword? As it is written, "For your sake we are being killed all day long; we are accounted as sheep to be slaughtered." No, in all these things we are more than conquerors through him who loved us. For I am convinced that neither death, nor life, nor angels, nor rulers, nor things present, nor things to come, nor powers, nor height, nor depth, nor anything else in all creation, will be able to separate us from the love of God in Christ Jesus our Lord. (Rom. 8:28, 31–39)

While in seclusion, I heard of the death of Bishop Dunstan Nsubuga's wife in a car accident.[6] I briefly emerged from my safe haven to attend the burial at Namirembe Cathedral.

---

6. The accident was deemed suspicious in light of the circumstances surrounding the death of the archbishop, who had allegedly died in a car accident.

Notwithstanding my faith, I became frightened when I learned of the violent death of Mr. Byron Kawadwa, a famous Ugandan playwright. Mr. Kawadwa had staged a musical drama, *Oluyimba lwa Wankoko*, with content critical of bad governance. Idi Amin was displeased. His agents abducted the playwright, allegedly dismembered him, and dumped his body by the banks of River Ssezibwa in Mukono District. Shaken, I prayed to God that if the dictator's agents were to find me, they may not chop me in pieces, but rather grant me a quick death.

At that critical moment of shaken trust, I made a vow to God to dedicate the next church on which I laid a foundation stone to St. Jude Thaddeus (Omutukuvu Yuda Saddayo), one of the twelve apostles, whose intercessory and healing powers for people in danger I had read about. Indeed, when I returned to my diocese, I dedicated a subparish church of Mayungwe Parish in Butambala to the saint. During my absence, Amin's agents kept coming to our home to ask about my whereabouts. When my wife, Mary, was asked what had befallen me, she simply responded that God knew ("Katonda Yamanyi"). I thank God for protecting and giving my wife and family the strength to withstand this difficult period.

The 1977 Centenary Celebrations

The archbishop was murdered just months before the church commemorated the Centenary of the Anglican Faith in Uganda. During the centenary celebrations, the church would also commemorate the witness of the famous Uganda martyrs whose steadfast loyalty to their faith in the face of Kabaka Mwanga's wrath led to their deaths in 1886, but strengthened the church. These martyrs were tied up and burnt on a pyre on orders of the king, who sensed that the new Christian faiths and their converts were undermining his authority.

In April 1977, the House of Bishops, led by Bishop Dunstan Nsubuga of Namirembe Diocese met and elected Bishop Silvanus Wani as a successor to Archbishop Luwum. Bishop Wani was from

Amin's home region, but he was freely elected by the bishops to be the next leader of the Church of Uganda.

The new archbishop was enthroned at Namirembe Cathedral on May 15, 1977, and on June 3, 1977, we celebrated the Centenary of the Anglican Church in Uganda. Strengthened by the example of Archbishop Luwum's martyrdom, Christians turned out in droves to churches to celebrate one hundred years of Christendom in Uganda. It was as if they were defying Amin's attempt to exterminate Christianity.

A Luganda song composed in commemoration of the Uganda martyrs and for use during the centenary celebrations had a particularly pertinent chorus:

"Alelluya, ku lwa Yesu, batibwa nga bayimba"

Alleluia, in the name of Jesus, they died praising him

"Bewayo Abaana bebazibwa, ku lwaffe bawayo obulamu ne byonna"

For our salvation, they gave up everything including their lives,
thanks to them.

It was sung with extra gusto, implicitly acknowledging the recent martyrdom of Archbishop Janani Luwum.

As in the case of the Uganda martyrs, the martyrdom of the archbishop further strengthened the church. Subsequent years saw the creation of many new dioceses in the country. At the time of the archbishop's death, there were thirteen dioceses; there are now thirty-four Anglican dioceses, with a total of over 10 million Anglican Christians.

The 1978 Lambeth Conference

The horrific murder of the archbishop alerted the world to the tyranny in Uganda. To soften his image, Idi Amin facilitated the Church of Uganda bishops' travel to the 1978 Lambeth Conference in England. When Archbishop Silvanus Wani informed us that the president had chartered a special plane to transport us to the United Kingdom, we were both surprised and afraid. With scarcely another option, we accepted the president's offer, although we knew he was against us. We put our plight in God's hands. The day of the flight, Amin invited us to a presidential lodge on the shores of Lake Victoria.

When we arrived, the president was busy attending to his garden. When he eventually came to greet us, he was charming. His mood swings were notorious, however: he could be charming one moment, and within seconds rage with frightening anger. On this occasion, he greeted us warmly, with a big smile. He humored us when he told us that he had ensured that the plane transporting us to England was in perfect mechanical condition, because "I do not want people to say that I killed the bishops travelling on it." He assigned three intelligence officers to accompany us. Their role was to spy on us during the Lambeth Conference. He was essentially putting us on notice to be careful about what we say while at the conference.

At the conference most deliberations touched on human rights, social and economic rights, and morality. We passed several resolutions, including resolution 3, which was particularly pertinent to the situation in Uganda at the time.

Resolution 3, 1–5, read:

1. We call on governments to uphold human dignity; to defend human rights, including the exercise of freedom of speech, movement, and worship in accordance with the United Nations Declaration of Human Rights; the right to be housed, freedom to work, the right to eat, the right to be educated; and to give human value and worth precedence over social and ethnic demarcations, regardless of sex, creed, or status;

2. We thank God for those faithful Christians who individually and collectively witness to their faith and convictions in the face of persecution, torture and martyrdom; and for those who work for and advocate human rights and peace among all peoples;

and we assure them of our prayers, as in penitence and hope we long to see the whole Church manifesting in its common life a genuine alternative to the acquisitiveness and division which surround it, and indeed penetrate it;

3. We pledge our support for those organizations and agencies which have taken positive stands on human rights, and those which assist with refugee problems;

4. We urge all Anglicans to seek positive ways of educating themselves about the liberation struggle of peoples in many parts of the world;

5. Finally we appeal to all Christians to lend their support to those who struggle for human freedom and who press forward in some places at great personal and corporate risk; we should not abandon them even if the struggle becomes violent. We are reminded that the ministry of the Church is to reveal the love of God by faithful proclamation of his Word, by sacrificial service, and by fervent prayers for his rule on earth.[7]

While at Lambeth we were surprised to hear Amin accusing the church of promoting homosexuality even though the issue was only tangentially discussed. We interpreted this accusation as yet another ploy to discredit and defame the church in order to pave the way for his theocratic Muslim state.

Sadly, my Aunt, Yudesi Nanyonga, passed away during my absence. Due to a lack of modern preservation methods in Uganda at the time, she was buried quickly. I was unable to attend her funeral at Kitti. I am grateful to Mr. William Lugobe, my neighbor and good friend, who purchased the coffin in which she was buried. Above all, I thank my wife, Mary, for the care and treatment she gave my aunt as she neared death. I am also grateful to all the persons who reached out to us at this moment to ensure her a fitting burial.

---

7. *http://www.lambethconference.org/resolutions/1978/1978-3.cfm.*

4

The Church, Politics, and Society

Sabbatical Leave: Going for Further Studies (1982-1983)

In 1982, Archbishop Silvanus Wani and the House of Bishops granted me a sabbatical to enable me to pursue a doctor of ministry degree in the United States of America. I was awarded a fellowship to study at Yale Divinity School in New Haven, Connecticut, where I resided as I pursued my doctorate at the Hartford Seminary in Hartford, Connecticut. I spent some of the time at Yale Divinity School auditing noncredit courses in marriage counseling and worship, but my doctorate studies were entirely at the Hartford Seminary.

In Hartford, Mr. Worth and Mrs. Louise Loomis generously hosted me. The Loomis's kindness and generosity enabled me to feel at home and so fueled my productivity that I completed my doctoral studies in a relatively short period of time. The Loomis family also offered to host my son, Joseph, after my return to Uganda. Due to the insecurity in Uganda at the time, we thought it advisable for Joseph to study in the United States, where he was born. The Loomis family, with the support of Rev. Hugh McCandless, generously supported Joseph through Salisbury School, a preparatory school in Connecticut, and Columbia College, the undergraduate division of Columbia University in New York City. I am eternally grateful to them.

I am also thankful for the support of my fellow bishops during my absence from family and the diocese. I delegated my diocesan administrative responsibilities to regents: Ven. Rev. Esawo

Sendiwala; Rev. Canon Erisa Wamala; Archdeacon, Rev. Semeon Ssemakula, and Canon Yokana Mukasa, a senior lay leader. I am grateful for the wonderful job they did.

During my sabbatical, bishops—Amos Bentugura of Ankole Diocese; Misaeri Kauma of Namirembe Diocese; and Lucas Gona-hasa, assistant bishop of Kampala—performed episcopal duties such as ordinations and confirmations on my behalf. Their assistance illustrated a simple truth: colleagues will help you if you trust them.

At the Hartford Seminary I studied marriage and divorce from a Christian, biblical perspective, particularly in contrast to the traditional African perspective.[1] My research confirmed my experience: in many African cultures, polygamy is so ingrained that it presents a challenge to the church's mission. For instance, some cultures mandate a son to take on his deceased brother's wife as a means to ensure security for the children. Thus I concluded that while the church rightly promotes monogamy as the ideal and only acceptable Christian marriage, it should not prevent circumstantial polygamists and their offspring from receiving the Good News according to Christ.

Isolating polygamists limits the reach of the gospel. I argued that the church paradoxically helps to perpetuate the traditional status quo by isolating the polygamists. Without the influence of the church's teachings, polygamists' offspring readily maintain the tradition.

Predictably, my recommendations caused controversy within the Church of Uganda. The church and Christians accused me of promoting polygamy; indeed, many women boycotted my services until I clarified my position.[2]

---

1. My unpublished dissertation was titled: "Polygamy, Monogamy and Divorce: A Biblical, Historical and African Perspective" (Hartford Seminary, 1983).

2. The current archbishop of the Church of Uganda, the Most. Rev. Stanley Ntagali, recently published a book (with Eileen Hodgetts) titled *More Than One Wife: Polygamy and Grace* (Emerge Publishing, 2013).

I shared my research on the subject at the 1988 Lambeth Conference in England. My views and those of others were incorporated into Lambeth Resolution 26, on the Church and Polygamy, which read:

> This Conference upholds monogamy as God's plan, and as the ideal relationship of love between husband and wife; it nevertheless recommends that a polygamist who responds to the Gospel and wishes to join the Anglican Church may be baptized and confirmed with his believing wives and children on the following conditions:
>
> (1) that the polygamist shall promise not to marry again as long as any of his wives at the time of his conversion are alive;
>
> (2) that the receiving of such a polygamist has the consent of the local Anglican community;
>
> (3) that such a polygamist shall not be compelled to put away any of his wives, on account of the social deprivation they would suffer;
>
> (4) and recommends that provinces where the Churches face problems of polygamy are encouraged to share information of their pastoral approach to Christians who become polygamists so that the most appropriate way of disciplining and pastoring to them can be found, and that the ACC be requested to facilitate the sharing of that information.[3]

My doctoral work also examined the implications of the concept of divorce in the church. I found that the marriage vow "until death do us part" has been abused. In fact, atrocities are sometimes committed by persons seeking to end their marriages. My studies convinced me of a need to expand the meaning of the "until death do us part" vow. Without love there is no relationship, and the lack of love in a relationship signifies a marriage's spiritual death.

---

3. *http://http://www.lambethconference.org/resolutions/1988/1988-26.cfm.*

In essence, where one or both parties in a marriage experience an irremediable lack of love, it could be said that death has parted the couple. It is not useful for the church to force Christians to stay in loveless marriages the effects of which have far-reaching implications on children. Rather, the church should seek ways to counsel separated couples to reach good Christian accommodations and reconciliation in the interest of raising wholesome children.

Church Politics and Society

I would be remiss not to mention the interrelationship of the church, politics, and society during my years of service. The church has at times been a voice for the poor and the oppressed, and has fostered reconciliation and peace, but, at other times, the church has been silent in times of great turmoil and suffering afflicting segments of society.

During and shortly after my studies at the Union Theological Seminary in the 1960s, there was great political turmoil in Uganda, which also found expression in the church. The modern nation of Uganda was a colonial creation. Prior to colonization, present-day Uganda consisted of independent political entities, the most prominent of which was the Buganda Kingdom. But most of modern Uganda, including Prime Minister Obote's region, had been under republican rule without kings. The notion of monarchical rule was anathema to them.

Beginning in 1964, there developed tension between the Buganda Kingdom led by the Kabaka (king) and the central government led by Prime Minister Milton Obote over "the lost counties," territories annexed to Buganda by the British from the rival Bunyoro Kingdom. After independence from the British, the new prime minister pursued a referendum (despite strong protests by the Kabaka and Buganda) for residents within the territories to decide whether to remain under the jurisdiction of Buganda, or return to Bunyoro. The ensuing referendum and the lost counties residents' decision to return to Bunyoro incensed the Buganda establishment and precipitated a major fallout between Buganda and the central government. In May 1966, Prime Minister Obote ordered forces led by Idi Amin to attack the Kabaka's palace. The king escaped to England, where he died three years later.

On September 8, 1967, the prime minister passed a Republican constitution that abolished kingdoms and terminated Buganda's federal status. The kingdom's parliamentary building and palaces were turned into military offices and army barracks. These actions by the central government created an environment of fear, hatred, and mistrust that soon impacted sentiments within the Church of Uganda.

Prime Minister Obote's actions turned him into a very unpopular figure, particularly in Buganda. By 1971, when General Idi Amin staged a coup, overthrowing the prime minister, many Ugandans, especially in Buganda, were fed up with Obote's dictatorial rule and welcomed the general with wild celebrations. However, Idi Amin soon turned tyrannical.

The events and the atmosphere leading to Obote's overthrow colored much of the interaction in Church of Uganda, particularly between the Buganda Dioceses of Namirembe and West Buganda and Anglican dioceses in the rest of the country.[4]

In March 1964, as Archbishop Leslie Brown, a Briton, prepared to retire, he appointed the Rev. Canon Dunstan Nsubuga, then dean of Namirembe, as his assistant bishop. At the time, the archbishop was also the bishop of Namirembe, the mother diocese of the Anglican church in Uganda. There was a strong expectation in Buganda that on Leslie Brown's retirement, Dunstan Nsubuga, who hailed from Buganda, would likewise become archbishop of

---

4. For a good discussion of the events narrated here, along with an excellent history of the church and its role in Uganda, read Bishop David Zac Niringiye's "The Church in the World: A Historical-Ecclesiological Study of the Church of Uganda with Particular Reference to Post-Independence Uganda, 1962–1992" (doctor of philosophy thesis, University of Edinburg, 1997). Dr. Niringiye recently served as assistant bishop of Kampala Diocese, but has since retired.

the entire Church of Uganda. But out of the nine dioceses that constituted the province of the Church of Uganda, Rwanda, Burundi, and Boga-Zaire, only two were Buganda dioceses.

In November 1965, Eric Sabiti, bishop of Rwenzori Diocese at Fort Portal, was elected archbishop by bishops of the Church of Uganda, except the two from Buganda. On January 25, 1966, he was enthroned as archbishop of the Church of Uganda at Namirembe Cathedral.

The constitution of the church at the time stipulated that the archbishop would preside over the church while remaining the bishop of the diocese he led at the time of his election. Yet the newly elected archbishop and the other non-Buganda bishops sought to amend the constitution to remove that stipulation. They argued that it would be very cumbersome for the archbishop to maintain and travel between two far-flung residences in the course of his duties, Fort Portal being 200 miles away from Namirembe in Kampala. They pointed out that while Namirembe was the headquarters of Namirembe Diocese, it was also the headquarters of the Church of Uganda.

They proposed a plan to build a residence and office for the archbishop at Namirembe. The Baganda, the indigenous ethnic group of Buganda, protested this plan. They interpreted it as an attempt by "foreigners" to take over the "Kabaka's Cathedral" just as the central government had confiscated the Buganda kingdom's properties, including the kingdom's parliamentary building (the Bulange), the king's palaces, and county administrative headquarters. They saw the attempt to relocate the archbishop to Namirembe as a ploy by Obote and his political kinsmen to further demoralize Buganda. Namirembe Diocese also rejected a compromise plan to carve a new Kampala Diocese from the Namirembe Diocese for the archbishop.

The political tension within the church culminated into an ugly incident on January 31, 1971: Bishop Dunstan Nsubuga invited Archbishop Eric Sabiti to preside over a thanksgiving service at Namirembe Cathedral, but when the archbishop arrived, he was locked out of the cathedral by a few overzealous Baganda Christians.

The Intervention of Idi Amin

Paradoxically, given his ensuing Islamic agenda, it was President Idi Amin, then a new ruler seeking to consolidate his support, who enabled the church to resolve the crisis. He appointed a secretary of religious affairs whose mandate was to seek and promote solutions to rifts that bedeviled religious institutions at the time, particularly among the Anglican Church of Uganda and the Uganda Muslim Council. In May 1971, the president directed all the Anglican bishops and their diocesan councils to meet him at Kabale to try and resolve the crisis. In November 1971, when it was clear that the two sides had failed to come to an agreement, Idi Amin proposed that since the rift in the church was caused by both the province's and Namirembe Diocese's headquarters being on the same hill, Namirembe Diocese's headquarters should relocate to a small town of Mukono (thirty-one miles away), while the province's headquarters remain at Namirembe. This brash proposal forced the two sides to seek a compromise. The Church of Uganda province wisely determined that a perception by Baganda Christians that they were forced out of Namirembe would cause irreparable disunity. The Buganda Dioceses on the other hand could not accept the loss of Namirembe. The creation of Kampala Diocese was a better alternative.[5]

Idi Amin's Regime: Hardship and New Beginnings

Notwithstanding his positive intervention into church affairs, Idi Amin soon attempted to erase Christianity from Uganda. When the United Kingdom, the United States, and Israel ceased to support him due to his extreme abuse of human rights, he allied Uganda with Saudi Arabia and Libya. He invited both King Faisal of Saudi Arabia and President Muamar Gaddafi of Libya on official visits. Gaddafi pledged to finance Amin's Islamization project. Archbishop Luwum boldly spoke up against this agenda.

---

5. Niringiye, "The Church in the World," 161.

In August 1972, Idi Amin announced that he had a dream in which God told him to expel the "Asians," largely Indians and some Pakistanis, about 70,000 people out of a total Ugandan population of between 5 and 6 million people. He followed through on his "dream." The Asians he expelled comprised of most of Uganda's industrialists, traders, artisans, and senior civil servants. They controlled large portions of the economy, including import-export trade, commerce, industry, and most of the retail sector. Amin allocated their businesses and properties to army and civilian cronies with neither experience to run them nor education.

As a result of the expulsion, many essential goods became scarce. Those of us who were able would drive all the way from Kampala to Nairobi, a distance of over 300 miles, in order to buy simple commodities like sugar, salt, and soap; but it was a blessing in disguise. Out of necessity, native Ugandans learned to be frugal and inventive. Many evolved into very successful businessmen, traders, and industrialists

As the regime became insecure due to threats from Tanzania-based rebels, it set up checkpoints manned by ruthless, menacing soldiers. I witnessed three incidents which may give readers some sense of the dread that citizens experienced at these checkpoints:

> On one occasion soldiers stopped my car; they ordered us out and inexplicably forced the driver to sit on the ground in the middle of the road. They threatened to shoot, but, suddenly without explanation, they nonchalantly waved us off. On another occasion, they stopped us shouting "Nyinyi maiti, nyinyi maiti" in Swahili (translation: "You are as good as dead"). But when they saw my episcopal attire, they let us proceed. Perhaps the most memorable encounter was a time when the soldiers stopped my car at a checkpoint. They demanded identification; unfortunately, a young priest who was travelling with me had left his identity card behind! The soldiers labeled him a terrorist; they were going to detain him. I tried to intercede on his behalf, but to no avail. Instinctively, I knew that if

we proceeded without him, the clergyman would not be seen alive
again. I told the soldiers that I could not leave the man of God
behind; I would rather they detained me along with him as they
awaited his identity card. Perhaps touched by the gesture, they
permitted all of us to proceed to our destination.

It was by God's grace that these encounters ended well. I am
inclined to believe that my bishopric cross and purple shirt were
the shields that God wielded to protect us. Many other Ugandans
did not fare so well in similar circumstances.

The Effects of the Chaotic Amin Period

In October 1978, Idi Amin annexed the Kagera salient region of
Tanzania, claiming that it belonged to Uganda. Tanzania, along
with Ugandan exile forces loyal to former Prime Minister Milton
Obote, responded by invading Uganda. On April 12, 1979, Idi
Amin fled to exile, first to Libya and then to Saudi Arabia. During
the war, citizens, such as us, in the path of the war were advised to
leave the zone of the conflict. My family and I sought refuge in our
native home area of Singo. My eldest son, Moses, chose to stay to
keep watch over our home, but, due to the intensity of the war, he
too eventually had to evacuate.

By the beginning of 1979, when there was a lull in the fighting,
I ventured back to my diocese, without my family, so that I could
lead Easter services at the cathedral. As I drove through Kampala
on my way to Masaka, I saw many dead bodies on the streets. I was
terrified; but, fortunately, no one stopped me.[6]

On arrival at the diocesan headquarters, I found our official
bishop's residence at Kako hill completely vandalized. The doors
and windows were shattered. All our belongings, including my
clerical robes, heirlooms, and family memorabilia that we had left

---

6. I have to confess that I drove at such a terrific speed that the journey from
Singo to Kako took me only three hours!

in the house had been looted. The house was completely bare. My wife and I slowly replenished our home, going all the way to Nairobi, in neighboring Kenya, to buy what we needed, as Uganda's economy was in complete shatters. Even essentials like sugar and salt could not be procured internally. Masaka's central business district had been completely razed to the ground by the invaders' cannons. Despite our loss, we were thankful to God for preserving our lives and for taking us out of harm's way.

In the period following Amin's overthrow, Ugandans experienced chaotic, indiscriminate violence on an unprecedented scale. Kampala environs and Idi Amin's home region of West Nile particularly suffered. The short-lived, ineffective figurehead governments of Yusufu Lule and Godfrey Lukongwa Binaisa that immediately followed Idi Amin's departure only served to pave way for the eventual return to power of Milton Obote.

During this interregnum in 1980, Godfrey Binaisa, one of the transitional presidents and son of my friend, the Rev. Canon Ananiya Binaisa, invited me for an overnight stay at the State House, the official residence of the president of Uganda. During my visit, I was impressed by the president's daily routine that prioritized prayer. And it was not an act to impress the bishop. I was told that the president invariably prayed before morning briefings by his press secretary who kept him abreast of national and worldwide events. The president was also keen on reading a variety of daily newspapers, which his press secretary provided. I was gratified to note that not only did the president entrust his leadership in God, but he also endeavored to stay independently informed beyond the din of advisors.

Pilgrimage to Israel

In 1980, soon after my visit with the president, I embarked on a group pilgrimage to Israel. I was excited to go see Jesus's native land. In Israel, we visited Bethlehem, Jesus's birthplace, and Nazareth, the humble village whence he was brought up.

In Nazareth, we also saw the cliff from which angry members of a synagogue intended to thrust Jesus to the valley below. And in the environs of Jerusalem, we observed the path of the cross, along which Jesus walked to his crucifixion on the hill of Golgotha. I marveled at the commitment and dedication to the remission of ours sins that Jesus exhibited by undertaking the arduous walk while laden with a heavy cross. And in old Jerusalem, we visited the empty sepulcher of the risen Christ.

Further, we saw the "Wailing Wall," part of the temple destroyed by Roman commander Titus (later emperor) in 70 CE during the first Jewish-Roman war. I was impressed by the wall's massive stones, weighing up to eight tons, which sit atop each other without any mortar. Another highlight of our pilgrimage was the journey we took from Jerusalem to Jericho to commemorate Jesus's famous parable of the Good Samaritan. The road to Jericho that we saw was steep, winding, and desolate. I could see why in Jesus's time it was a safe haven for bandits.

I reflected on the story of the Good Samaritan when we visited the Holocaust Museum, which serves as a reminder of the Jewish holocaust. Where were the Good Samaritans as Hitler suffocated Jews in gas chambers?

A similar genocide occurred in Rwanda in 1994 when between 500,000 and 1 million citizens of Rwanda were murdered by their neighbors in a mere 100 days.[7] The killers dumped the victims into the Kagera River, which flows into Lake Victoria. Their bodies floated through the river all the way to Uganda. I remember praying for countless mutilated bodies of victims that washed ashore at Kansensero landing site in Rakai District. The experience was deeply traumatic.

There is a need for Good Samaritans (world powers and governments in addition to individuals) to intervene on behalf of the

---

7. Uganda has also suffered periods of genocide during the regime of Idi Amin, and in subsequent dictatorships.

persecuted, the oppressed, and the subjugated wherever and whomever they maybe. Instead of investing colossal sums of money in destructive weapons, world leaders should deploy unconditional, brotherly love which engenders compassion, forgiveness, and reconciliation.

In Galilee, we visited the mountain of blessing where Jesus shared his divine wisdom with multitudes (Matt. 5:1). We also visited Cana, where Jesus turned water into abundant wine for wedding guests to enjoy. I could imagine their joy.

Unfortunately, some take Jesus's provision of wine as a license to drink without limits. But we only glorify God when we eat and drink in moderation. In 1 Corinthians 10:31, St. Paul says: "so, whether you eat or drink, or whatever you do, do everything for the glory of God." Drunkenness and diseases stemming from overindulgence do not reflect God's glory.

And in 1 Corinthians 3:16–17, St Paul asks: "Do you not know that you are God's temple and that God's Spirit dwells in you? If anyone destroys God's temple, God will destroy that person. For God's temple is holy, and you are that temple." By overindulging in food and drink, we destroy God's temple—ourselves. Moreover, Proverbs 23:20–21 warns us that gluttonous drinking and eating lead to miserly:

> Do not be among winebibbers,
>> or among gluttonous eaters of meat;
> for the drunkard and the glutton will come to poverty,
>> and drowsiness will clothe them with rags.

Unfortunately many of our fellow citizens of the world do not enjoy Cana-like abundance. They suffer the opposite of overindulgence: starvation. Indeed, as I was enjoying the pilgrimage to Israel, the semiarid Karamoja region of Uganda was beset by a severe famine in which between 20,000 and 50,000 people (mostly children)—14 percent of its population then—are said to have died.

As beings created in the image of God, we should emulate Jesus at Cana; we should harness our resources to ensure that no human beings die of hunger or thirst.

The failure to ensure adequate food and water for all in Uganda is largely due to bureaucratic incompetence and indifference. While Karamoja is semiarid, Uganda as a whole is mostly blessed with ample rainfall and fertile soils. Authorities have not adequately facilitated planning for the periodic droughts. Moreover, government authorities in Uganda have perennially underinvested in agriculture; extension services, irrigation, storage, and distribution systems are either underdeveloped, or in some areas, nonexistent. Worse still, cooperative societies, through which farmers marketed, transported, and distributed their produce, collapsed due to political intervention and corruption.

Malnutrition and obesity due to a lack of proper eating guidelines are quite rampant. Diabetes, high blood pressure, and heart disease are becoming increasingly common among middle-class Ugandans, who are increasingly eating processed foods and drinks, despite the fact that Uganda is blessed with a great variety of nutritious, organic food. There is a need for Ugandan authorities to educate families not only about the nutritional content of widely available foodstuffs, but also on the impact of proper nutrition in the growth and health of children. Accurate nutritional labeling of processed foodstuffs should also be enforced. Churches and mosques, as stewards of God's temple, should partner with the government to give guidance to the population concerning proper nutrition, especially for the children and pregnant mothers. They should also use their countrywide networks in partnership with the government to ensure that food is distributed to areas of need.

The Trauma of the Post-Amin Civil War

In 1980, the pro-Obote military commission organized elections, which were widely perceived to be rigged in favor of Milton

Obote's Uganda People's Congress, U.P.C, at the expense of the Democratic Party (D.P.). On the pretext of the "rigged" elections, General Yoweri Museveni, the current president, declared a guerilla war on Obote's "elected" government. The resulting civil war led to a great number of deaths both in Buganda and subsequently, in northern Uganda.

The climax of the worst atrocities of the war found me once again in the United States pursuing my doctorate at the Hartford Seminary. Even though my wife and children were not in the operational zone of the war, the war intimately affected us. My elderly mother, who craved her independence, decided to stay at her home in Singo, which eventually got enveloped in the war. In 1983, my younger brother, Langton Ganafa, went to take care of her. Government forces suspected my brother of supporting the antigovernment rebels; they shot him dead in the compound of my mother's house, right in front of her. This brutal act traumatized my mother. By the grace of God, and with the assistance of Martini, her resident grandson, she garnered the strength and courage to carry Langton's bleeding body into her living room. My mother prayed for Langton's soul, and then the two of them dug a shallow grave, buried the body, and covered the grave with stones. Langton was only forty-two. In 1990, after my mother's death, I exhumed his remains and reburied them in a deeper grave marked with a tombstone.

On my return from the United States in 1983, I set out to rescue my mother from the danger of the war zone. I narrowly escaped death at the hands of unruly soldiers at checkpoints. It was not easy to find my mother as many villages, including hers, were deserted. But on the second day of my search, I found her at Kyanuna village on Hoima Road. She was dressed in rags, with her hair and nails overgrown like those of a bush woman. I am very grateful to Rev. Anne Gariyo, one of my former students at Bishop Tucker Theological College, who offered my mother a dress to replace the rags she was wearing.

Contrasting Fortunes during the Yoweri Museveni Years

I thanked God when there was a change of government in 1986. The new president, General Yoweri Kaguta Museveni, brought with him "The Ten Point Program," a manifesto that captured our imagination as it emphasized human rights, democracy, freedom of speech, and the rule of law. In Buganda and in much of the country, the new government's army was perceived as more disciplined and more cordial with the civilian population. In addition, the new government implemented a political system that encouraged people to directly participate in local political affairs.

And, after negotiations with clan and religious leaders in Buganda, President Museveni enabled the return of the crown prince of Buganda. The crown prince was later enthroned as the 36th king of Buganda, His Majesty Ronald Muwenda Mutebi II.[8] His ascendance to the throne was gratifying to us in Buganda and stoked our hope that a federal system of governance that would grant Uganda's regions a level of economic and political autonomy was imminent.

However, some of the new government's reforms soon became controversial. In my diocese, the business class complained about what they regarded as socialist tendencies of the new government. Their unease was sparked by the new rulers' decision to employ barter trade, which involved exchanging Uganda's agricultural produce such as coffee and foodstuffs for oil and other commodities from Libya and Cuba. Others complained of the confiscation of their farms and cattle by government authorities.

Further, the government's decision to devalue the shilling against the dollar in an effort to combat the black market depleted many people's savings, as their holdings were suddenly a fraction of their former value. One of my friends who had deposited five

---

8. The king is a constitutional monarch. Administrative authority lies in his prime minister, the Katikkiro.

hundred million shillings was left with only three and a half million shillings after the devaluation of the shilling.

When the government adopted structural adjustment reforms per International Monetary Fund (IMF) and World Bank prescriptions, many civil servants lost their jobs. Others amassed great wealth as they acquired formerly public properties and businesses that were privatized by the government.

In rural areas, these tough reforms coincided with the termination of cooperative societies that had enabled subsistence farmers to market their produce and the emergence of destructive pests that destroyed banana and coffee plantations that the rural population in my diocese depended on for food and sustenance. An unprecedented level of poverty emerged in Buganda's rural areas. In the meantime, the city of Kampala became vibrant with unprecedented economic activity.

Sadly, some business and government elites decided to exploit the desperate poverty in the countryside; they dispossessed the peasants of the one resource that provided them some economic security: their land, which they bought at give-away rates. On witnessing the hopeless situation in the villages, many youth migrated to the city and surrounding towns, only to end up in mushrooming slums with the most decrepit, unsanitary conditions. This created a situation ripe with insecurity, as armed robberies and intermittent riots became a norm.

During this period, thugs invaded our official residence. They came while shooting, perhaps, to cow us. On hearing the shots, our two unarmed watchmen and even our dog fled for dear life! The thugs broke into our bedroom. When I asked one masked fellow why he wanted to kill me, he told me that he had not come to kill me; he was only after the money which he knew I had. I told him that I did not have any money. He ransacked the drawers, but found no money. By God's providence, I had just transferred the new cathedral fund's collections, gathered on pastoral parish visits, to the diocesan treasurer. The man inquired if my wife had money, but Mary had hidden in the living room. He opened the living room's door, but did not see Mary as she was hiding behind one of the sofas. Having failed to find any money, the invaders left hurriedly, without harming us or taking anything. It was God's hand that protected us.

The Church's Voice during the Turmoil of the Post-Amin Period

Church leaders are human beings who are largely conditioned and influenced by the politics, biases, and human condition of the environment in which they reside. Therefore it is incumbent upon Christians to be active participants in church affairs, so that they can call the church to account when it falls short in its mission as a bearer of Christ's Good News to the afflicted, the oppressed, and the marginalized. As the example of Archbishop Janani Luwum illustrates, the church, as the embodiment of the love of Jesus, needs to speak out actively against political and economic excesses, even at the highest of costs.

Unfortunately, with a few exceptions, the response of the Church of Uganda to injustice and tyranny has often mirrored the dominant attitudes and biases within the population. While Idi Amin was massacring Acholi and Langi army personnel in 1971, the church leadership, with the exception of the bishops of northern Uganda, was slow to speak out.

During the post-Amin turmoil in West Nile and in Buganda, the province of the Church of Uganda under the leadership of Archbishop Yona Okoth, a close associate of President Milton Obote, hardly spoke out against the atrocities.

In 1981, a Kakwa religious leader, Archbishop Silvanus Wani from West Nile and four other clerics from Buganda: Bishop Dunstan Nsubuga, the Anglican bishop of Namirembe Diocese; Cardinal Emmanuel Nsubuga, the head of the Catholic Church in Uganda; Chief Khadi Kassim Mulumba, the leader of Muslims in Uganda; and Archbishop Theopodos Nankyama, the primate of the Orthodox Church in Uganda, wrote a letter to President Obote, which was reminiscent of the one we wrote to Idi Amin years earlier.

Here is an excerpt from their letter:

> The security situation has gone from bad to worse. The groaning, tears, sighs and the pains of the people of Uganda, especially in Arua and around Kampala, have forced us to seek an appointment with you, to bring to your notice our own experience, to discuss with you and to suggest ways and means of solving the problem.
>
> The Uganda you lead is bleeding to death. It needs a Good Samaritan to give it first aid and treatment and healing. The tears that people around Kampala, especially at Kapeeka, Semuto, Wakiso, Kakiri, Matuga, Namanve, Luwero and Wobulenzi are shedding, have reached a quantity that should force those who lead to stop, listen to God, and examine their principles and have more compassion over those that are suffering and many that have lost their lives.
>
> What the people around Kampala are going through is very much like what is going on in West Nile. For within three weeks, a total of over a hundred innocent citizens of Uganda, men, women, children and old people have been murdered mainly by the gun and by people who are there to protect and defend the citizens of Uganda.
>
> We have no objections to operations made by the army to search for guns if they have enough evidence but we strongly object to the way it is done. Once they are sent in an area, they start shooting innocent people without discrimination. Property is looted, women and girls are raped, and many civilians desert their homes to save their lives. Thus the reputation of the army has been greatly damaged among the people. They can no longer trust them. As soon as they appear on site they run away.[9]

---

9. Niringiye, "The Church in the World," 245–46.

As a consequence of the suffering at the hands of the armed forces mostly recruited from the northern regions of the country during Idi Amin's and Obote's two regimes, there developed an unfortunate stereotype of people from the north as evil, dangerous, and murderous. Many Baganda genuinely developed a fear and loathing of "northerners." The church recognized a need for reconciliation in the name of Jesus Christ.

During Namirembe Diocese's mission of 1988, with a theme of reconciliation, Bishop Kauma of Namirembe, whose diocese was hard-hit by army atrocities, invited Bishop Milchisedek Otim of Lango, President Obote's home region in northern Uganda, to give the keynote speech at the end of the mission's service at Namirembe. This gesture began the process of reconciliation between the north and Buganda within the church.

Reflecting on the occasion, my friend, the late Bishop Kauma recounted thus:

> When he [Melchisedek Otim] came, God had convicted many of us about the hatred we had against anybody from the north, simply because they were the leaders. I mean, Obote was a northerner, and most of the soldiers were northerners. So in short it was the northerners who were killing our people, who had led Uganda to backwardness; . . . we had a wholesale hatred for anything they did. . . .
>
> But God spoke to me about this and said this is a wrong assertion. "You cannot blame people like that wholesale. . . ."
>
> So when Melchisedek was coming, I said, "I cannot look at him just as somebody from the north, when we've been together, we are both bishops and brethren." And God said, "You are a brother and he is a brother," and then God showed me that what many northerners did is not restricted to them. . . . It is the sinful nature that we all share. . . .
>
> So it was not a tribe; it was not an ethnic sin. It was a human problem.

And I said that since I could not call all the Baganda, I said [to Melchisedek] on behalf of the Baganda who live in Namirembe Diocese, "I just want to say sorry about the things the Baganda did for (to) the northerners."[10]

The two bishops embraced one another before the mammoth congregation in the cathedral and Otim also repented on behalf of Obote and the Langi for the ills against the Baganda. Referring to the impact of this moment on his attitude toward the northerners, Kauma commented, "It is amazing. I have never looked at northerners after repentance in the same way I did before repentance (sic). When I meet them, they are my brethren. They can be bad people just like there are bad Baganda; but not just because they are northerners."[11]

The oneness of all human beings without regard to ethnicity, race, or religion that Bishop Kauma expressed so well was further revealed to me when in 2000, the Rt. Rev. Dr. Enock Drati, bishop of Idi Amin's home region of West Nile and Madi, invited me to conduct confirmation services on his behalf while he was sick. I accepted the invitation and tried to learn a few words in Lugbara, the language of the region. I was especially keen to learn greetings and words that the local church used during confirmation services. My intention was to ensure that confirmation candidates felt comfortable. The local Christians were grateful and referred to me as their rescuer in the time of need, particularly since I had travelled 300 miles by road from Kampala to be with them. They named me "Amabe." One Lugbara man told me that he was going to name his new-born son after me: Senyonjo.[12] I would love to see my

---

10. Niringiye, "The Church in the World," 261–62.

11. Niringiye, "The Church in the World," 262.

12. Each of the ethnic groups in Uganda is identified with a set of names of which they are very proud. Thus when a person from another ethnic group chooses to give his/her child your name, it is doubly a great honor and a sign of respect and affection.

namesake today. I hope he grew up to be a fine young man. I am grateful for the great generosity and hospitality that Bishop Drati and the parishioners in his diocese extended to me.

The Church of Uganda at Present

It is sad to note that we bishops failed to quickly come to terms with the suffering of the people of northern and northeastern Uganda as a result of the Kony insurgency and the government's "mopping up" operations. Kony, a former Catholic catechist, exploited the grievances of the people of northern Uganda whom Museveni had removed from power, some of whom reportedly suffered physical humiliation by the victors, to start an insurgency allegedly based on the Ten Commandments. He named his group "the Lord's Resistance Army (LRA)." The government operations included herding the local population into overcrowded camps where many died of disease and hunger. The operations were designed to isolate Kony from the population, and to deny him sustenance. Many people who stayed out of the camps got caught in the crossfire.

This time it was the bishops of northern Uganda that spoke out on behalf of the people, but the church leadership as a whole was largely mute. Many of us could not imagine that the government that had brought the peace we were enjoying could possibly be negligent in the protection and security of our northern brethren.

As the current government consolidated its power, there were restrictions on political party activities and allegations of rigged elections, but the church has only occasionally spoken out. There is a sense by observers that church leaders have been compromised by politicians through donations to church projects, and particularly through the current president's practice of donating new vehicles to newly consecrated bishops. It has been alleged that such gifts "buy" the church's voice.

In an environment of extreme deprivation, it has proven difficult to dissuade bishops from accepting "donations" from the government, which are supposedly given to "facilitate" their work. The exception was Bishop Mesusera Bugimbi of the Luwero Diocese who, on enthronement, declined to accept such a donation. We need prayers to stay on God's path despite earthly temptations and inducements.

5

Retirement, Reflection, and the Call to a New Ministry

SAYING FAREWELL TO THE CHRISTIANS of my diocese was hard and emotional. On February 28, 1998, having already exceeded the mandatory retirement age of sixty-five, I retired. I had served the Church of Uganda for thirty-five years in various capacities as deacon, theology teacher, priest, Bible translator, dean of the province, and as bishop.

During my twenty-four years of service as bishop of West Buganda Diocese, Masaka had become home. I had acquired some land and built there. But I decided to retire to my home in Bukoto, Kampala, over ninety miles away, in order to give a new bishop space to establish his administration without undue interference.

I am grateful for the opportunity that God gave me as bishop to nurture and expand the Christian community through baptisms, confirmations, ordinations, and marriage ceremonies.

MARRIAGES AND BAPTISMS

As bishop I married over 240 couples, whom Mary and I would someday like to invite for a thanksgiving service in celebration of God's grace that has enabled them to uphold this important institution. Even though priests and deacons conduct most of the baptisms in the church, I occasionally baptized children, especially those of couples whose weddings I had officiated. In all, I baptized over 750 babies.

Before I was enthroned as bishop, the church did not grant babies born out of wedlock the baptism sacrament. Some clergy were reprimanded for privately baptizing such babies. To reconcile my conscience with the church's position, I meditated on our Lord Jesus Christ's words as recorded in Mark 10:13–16:

> People were bringing little children to him in order that he might touch them; and the disciples spoke sternly to them. But when Jesus saw this, he was indignant and said to them, "Let the little children come to me; do not stop them; for it is to such as these that the kingdom of God belongs. Truly I tell you, whoever does not receive the kingdom of God as a little child will never enter it." And he took them up in his arms, laid his hands on them, and blessed them.

I concluded that it was wrong to deny any babies with Christian parents and sponsors baptism. Thus, in my diocese I encouraged baptism of all babies without discrimination. I am glad to say that the Church of Uganda as a whole eventually sanctioned the baptism of all babies with Christian godparents.

CONFIRMATIONS

One of the most significant moments in a Christian's life is one's confirmation of faith in Jesus Christ. I am very happy to note that I confirmed over 170,000 souls during my twenty-four-year tenure as bishop of the West Buganda Diocese. I always urged confirmation candidates to ask for the gift of the Holy Spirit to guide them, as they would hence be Christ's ambassadors. They would be living representations of the temple of God. No other "gods" would have power over them. I am gratified that during my travels—even recently in New York City—that I occasionally run across men and women who fondly tell me that I confirmed them. I pray to God that the Christians I confirmed remain Christ's ambassadors in whatever calling they chose for themselves.

ORDINATIONS

During my service as bishop of West Buganda, I ordained over two hundred clergy, most of whom are still living. Among the clergy I ordained is the recently deceased bishop of West Buganda, the Rt. Rev. Godfrey Makumbi, and his diocesan secretary, the Rev. Canon Samuel Mwesigwa. I cannot mention all of them here, but many of them currently have important leadership roles. One of them, Rev. Jackson Kasozi Nsamba, is currently the prime minister of Bunyoro Kingdom. Others are serving as head teachers, chaplains, university tutors, theologians, pastors, and parish priests. One of them, Rev. Isaac Nsereko, has built a great educational complex that educates, counsels, and nurtures disadvantaged children into useful, productive citizens.

I am grateful to clergy who inspired me and became close confidants. Among them are Rev. Edward Kambugu, who helped me secure a plot in Rakai Township; Rev. Canon Erasmus Nsamba, who effectively served as chaplain and accomplished many errands on my behalf; and Rev. Florence Namala, whose dedication to ministry, even when the church barred women's ordination, was inspirational. Her patience and faith in God were rewarded when the Anglican Church in Uganda eventually authorized the ordination of women. Florence is now officially a priest in the church. Mary and I would also like to salute the Rev. Knaack Jasper Kyeyune, who efficiently served as my diocesan secretary, and became a close confidant of ours in times of great stress.

Postretirement Service

At retirement in 1998, I still had enough energy and mental clarity to accomplish more in the service of God. I was concerned about the rampant deforestation taking place as a result of a rapid growth of the construction sector in Uganda. I consulted with leaders in my home village to persuade them to encourage people to plant trees. On my part, I planted fruit-bearing trees at my village home.

On reflection, I reconsidered the direction of my postretirement life. I had spent the vast majority of my life in service of people, both as a priest and as a counselor. I decided to continue along that path. At my age, I lacked the vigor of youth necessary for forestry!

Since my time as a deacon, I had gravitated toward Christian counseling. And during my doctoral studies at the Hartford Seminary, I audited counseling classes at Yale Divinity School. I was particularly interested in pastoral issues concerning marriage and human sexuality within a Christian context.

Consequently, as part of my post retirement service, I established a counseling service on Kisingiri Road in the Mengo suburb of Kampala. I provided Christian counseling to couples, singles, youth, and to anyone who needed counseling. I assured my counselees of privacy, confidentiality, respect, understanding, and freedom of expression.

I provided counseling to the youth and the unemployed free of charge, but charged a small fee to those who could afford it. Since I was convinced that counseling should be available for all who needed it, I solicited for donations to facilitate universal access to my services. Fellow bishops and the church, as a whole, appreciated my services and supported my work. In addition to counseling, I would often fill in for the bishops when requested.

Advocacy for the Equal Treatment of Lesbian, Gay, Bisexual, Transgender, and Queer (LGBTQ) Persons

One day in December 2000, while at my counseling office, the Rev. Eric Kasirye approached me with a request to provide counseling to a few disenchanted young people who felt marginalized by the church and society. I acceded to his request. In January 2001, he brought them to me for counseling. This was my first official encounter of LGBTQ persons in Uganda. On listening to the young men, I realized that they were despondent and frightened.

In one session, a young gay man narrated to me a litany of tribulations: his parents had rejected him; his peers did not understand him and the church had commanded him to change from his "devil-ish" ways. The pastor to whom he had gone for prayer told him to "change to a Christian life." The young man prayed and fasted for thirty days, but he could not alter his sexual inclination toward fellow males. The pastor told him that if he did not change, he was destined to go to hell. He wondered why God had created him if he was destined to go to hell. He was at a loss, even contemplating suicide.

On listening to the young man, I advised him to accept himself. I assured him that God, who created all of us in his own image, loved him.

Following my assurance that I would not vilify LGBTQ persons, Rev. Kasirye, the young clergyman who introduced me to the LGBTQ community and a member of Integrity Uganda, an Episcopal LGBT Human Rights Advocacy group, requested that I accept an appointment to be chairman of Integrity Uganda. I accepted, not realizing at the time the extent of the Anglican Church of Uganda's homophobia.

Around the same time, in early 2001, I travelled to the United States to attend a conference on behalf of an organization called Women and Youth Services (WAYS) of which I was patron. WAYS's mission was to empower and educate women and youth through the provision of vocational education and practical skills.

To my surprise in March 2001, while I was still in the United States, elements within the church, the government, and civil society accused me of promoting homosexuality. They directed that instead of counseling LGBT persons, I should encourage them to repent and to convert to heterosexuality. I knew that this was not right. Moreover, Jesus's call to his disciples was to preach the good news of salvation to all without discrimination. In the gospel Jesus reached out to everyone, including the prostitute. I therefore resolved that I could not abandon the LGBTQ community, in spite of the authorities' disapproval.

However, it grieved me deeply when a number of my colleagues and friends furiously turned against me; though in my heart, I still loved them. I prayed that God grant them the magnanimity to listen to and empathize with LGBTQ persons.

As I reflected on the situation, I composed the following:

A Prayer for Listening

O Listening God, thank you for being the perfect listener
Although you are communicating to us without ceasing,
Forgive us for not listening to you all the time,

Teach us, O God, to be good listeners,
Teach us to listen in silence,
In order to respond appropriately to others

Let us listen to you, the perfect listener.
Let us listen to our spouses,
Let us listen to the small and the great
Let us listen to the servants, the children, and the bosses
Let us listen to the inner voice within us
Let us listen to our workmates
Let us listen to our friends and our enemies
Let us listen to the marginalized excluded people
Teach us, O Lord, to listen to all peoples
In order to appreciate who they are, how they feel and what they value
May the Comforter, the Holy Spirit, guide us as we listen, now and
    forever more Amen.

As I prayed and reflected, I realized that I was only able to stand firm in the face of vehement opposition to my ministry to LGBTQ persons due to a conviction that God has sent me to bring good news to all, including the marginalized LGBTQ people created in God's own image, as are all of us. I have been privileged to listen face-to-face to experiences of gay and lesbian Christians. I am convinced that they did not choose to be born homosexual. They need to be listened to and welcomed into God's merciful hands rather than be discarded as outcasts. I can say that the truth has made me free, as it is written in John 8:32. Truth, compassion, and love are my guiding stars while serving all God's children. I believe in the universal God of compassion and love. He is the true almighty God above all others. I have found the Bible as a source of guidance. Reading the biblical texts in relation to contexts has been a useful tool as I apply it to the mistreated LGBTQ people in many of our churches and communities. The Bible should not be used as a weapon to punish the LGBTQ people.[1]

In May 2001, the Namirembe Diocesan Council met in the New Synod Hall and passed some resolutions condemning me for "promoting homosexuality."

The resolutions read as follows:

1. Homosexuality

   (a) Bishop Christopher Senyonjo's involvement in the promotion of homosexuality:

   The council learnt with profound shock, Bishop Christopher Senyonjo's involvement in the promotion of homosexuality in Uganda and abroad and has therefore resolved as follows:

   (i) To condemn Bishop Senyonjo's attitude and behavior towards homosexuality

   (ii) To debar with immediate effect Bishop Senyonjo from preaching, leading services, baptism, confirmation, addressing Christian congregations, solemnizing marriages, funeral services, moving in liturgical processions or any other act related with worship in the Diocese of Namirembe.

   (iii) To appeal to the Archbishop of the Province of the Church of Uganda to see to it that Bishop Christopher

---

1. It is important to note that while transcribing God's words, the authors of the various books in the Bible were steeped in particular cultural contexts; conceivably their biases (against particular minorities and practices) got intertwined with religious proscriptions.

> Senyonjo appears before the provincial tribunal and eventually be defrocked.

(b) Other homosexuals and promoters of homosexuality

> The council further resolves that:

> (i) All Christians of the Church of Uganda who will be found practicing or promoting homosexuality shall be denied Christian burial and other church rites, in the Diocese of Namirembe

> (ii) The Diocese to launch a vigorous crusade against all forms of homosexuality

> These resolutions were endorsed and signed by:

> Rev. Canon Nelson Kaweesa
> Diocesan Secretary

> The Rt. Rev. Samuel Ssekkadde
> Bishop of Namirembe
> Namirembe Diocesan Office

As I read the resolutions, I was perplexed by the extreme vitriol that the issue of homosexuality aroused within the church. I realize now that homophobia emanates from ignorance; we cannot dispel it until human sexuality in all its variances is openly discussed in all educational institutions, including theological seminaries.

Following the outcry, the director of WAYS asked me to relinquish my position as patron of the organization and completely disassociated from me. Though hurt by her decision, I did not fault her; my advocacy for LGBT human rights could have jeopardized the status of her organization.

Due to the cruel and frightening accusations against me, I felt it would not be safe for me to return to Uganda at the time. I extended my stay in the United States with the support and encouragement of friends. I am grateful to the Rev. Michael Hopkins and Mr. John Clinton Bradley who sheltered me at their home in Maryland for six months (March to September 2001).

During this dark period, Desmond Tutu, the eminent Anglican archbishop of South Africa and great man of God, sent me words of encouragement by email in 2001:

> I write to assure you of my support for your position, and to assure you of my prayers in the very difficult situation that you find yourself in as a result of your principled stance. Please feel free to make public the fact that I support you.

Emboldened, on May 14, 2001, I wrote a letter to the Anglican Church of Uganda in response to the resolutions.

> Although I am straight and not a promoter of homosexuality, I recognize that homosexuality is a fact. This I discovered when I was doing research for my doctorate at Yale University and at the Hartford seminary, and again as I counseled a number of people.
>
> People may differ as to how to deal with homosexuality, but this difference should not lead to animosity among Christians. It grieves me deeply that a number of good friends of mine have turned angrily against me. On my part, I love them still, and wish them no ill. Let us continue to be on speaking terms.
>
> Many people who profess to love Jesus have been known to commend harsh treatment to homosexuals in the name of the Bible, or God and his son, Jesus Christ! The words of our Lord Jesus Christ in John 16:12 have helped me as I face difficult situations day by day. "I have yet many things to say to you, but you can not bear them now." As Christians we are enjoined by our Lord and Savior to love one another, John 15:12.
>
> At this point, I appeal to all believers in God to remember that God is love. So in the name of God of Love, let nobody intimidate or harass my wife, my children, or my extended family because of this ministry I am called to do. . . .
>
> It has been alleged by some authorities in the Church that I intend to go around schools, and maybe churches as well, promoting homosexuality. This is not true. These kinds of rumors are

spread to soil my name. I respect the family unit and the hetero-sexuality of individuals, as I am also heterosexual.

As it is pointed out in one of the pamphlets entitled "HIV/AIDS in Uganda," published in September 2000 by the Uganda Aids Commission, it is necessary to accept that there are some homosexuals (page 5) in Uganda who need help in order to prevent contraction of HIV/AIDS. And those already living with HIV/AIDS are entitled to being given the same treatment as that we give to heterosexuals . . .

St. Paul is my mentor and a good example in my ministry. His ministry after meeting the Lord on his way to Damascus was not easy. But he tried to understand the Jews, the Gentiles and the weak, so that more of them may not be made to feel that they are excluded from salvation by Jesus Christ (1 Corinthians 9). I know that I didn't seek being called to this ministry. It is the Lord that sent that young priest to speak to me. It is the Lord Jesus Christ who chose me, John 15:16–17. Since I began my ministry in West Buganda Diocese in 1974, God has called me to the Ministry of Reconciliation—2 Corinthians 5:11–6:2. I am not doing this ministry for the sake of money, though I trust that God will not allow me to starve.

I conclude by emphasizing the fact that my role in this ministry is to provide a listening and counseling ear to the stigmatized, the rejected, the confused, the misunderstood, those who are regarded as the scum and outcasts of the world. But the church should remember that we are in the world, but we are not of the world, John 15:19. Christ is above our cultures. . . .

Witch hunting and the discrimination of people different from us hinder progress. How long is this going to last? The world has suffered enough. Enough is enough. Hate is the hell of the world. Love is the hope of the world. May the love of God and humanity fill the universe in this 21st century.

The terrorist attacks on New York and Washington, DC, on September 11, 2001, occurred while I was in the United States. As I reflected on the tragedy, I concluded that unless there was a great turn-about, our world is destined for destruction. This is because human sentiments of hatred, fear, and self-righteousness lead to all kinds of discrimination and atrocities. The attacks enabled me to contextualize my situation; I concluded that we should not be paralyzed by fear.

Soon after the attacks, I decided to return to Uganda. I was ready to answer any charges the church or the government could bring against me. I flew to Entebbe via Geneva by Swiss Airlines. I was scheduled to arrive at Entebbe Airport in Uganda during daytime, but in Geneva the pilot detected a fault in the plane just before take-off. We left three hours later and landed at Entebbe under cover of darkness. I disembarked the plane not knowing whether hostile government agents were waiting to arrest me. There were none.

My family fetched me from the airport. My wife, who had endured all sorts of innuendos due to my stance, was extremely happy to see me. We reached home before dawn and I rested.

Two days after my return, I ventured out into the streets of Kampala. A few people taunted me and hurled insults at me, including: "There goes a man who promotes homosexuality." I ignored them and the insults eventually subsided. To my relief, no official charges were instituted against me. But the church was evidently not done with me.

On January 24, 2002, the House of Bishops summoned me. The bishops now accused me of deviating from the 1998 Lambeth Conference's Resolutions regarding homosexuality.[2] On reading the resolutions, it is clear that this accusation was not quite accurate because Lambeth Resolution I.10, parts c and d below, stated thus regarding homosexuality:

This conference:

    c. recognizes that there are among us persons who experience themselves as having a homosexual orientation. Many of these

---

2. I did not attend the 1998 Lambeth Conference, as I had just retired.

are members of the Church and are seeking the pastoral care, moral direction of the Church, and God's transforming power for the living of their lives and the ordering of relationships. We commit ourselves to listen to the experience of homosexual persons and we wish to assure them that they are loved by God and that all baptized, believing and faithful persons, regardless of sexual orientation, are full members of the Body of Christ;

d. while rejecting homosexual practice as incompatible with Scripture, calls on all our people to minister pastorally and sensitively to all irrespective of sexual orientation and to condemn irrational fear of homosexuals, violence within marriage and any trivialization and commercialization of sex.[3]

I confidently informed the House of Bishops that all accusations against me were false. I also expressed surprise that my successor as bishop of West Buganda had threatened Christians to the effect that if they received me in their homes, they would be excommunicated. The bishop even contemplated passing a resolution to rescind all the sacraments such as confirmations and ordinations that I had performed during my twenty-four years of service in the diocese!

I told the House of Bishops that such a draconian response besmirched of donatism, which was rejected by the Universal Catholic Church. I requested that the House of Bishops appoint a special committee to grant me a hearing. The Rt. Rev. Ernest Shalita, bishop of Muhabura Diocese, supported my request. A committee of three bishops: the Rt. Rev. Dr. Eustace Kamanyire, bishop of Rwenzori Diocese; the Rt. Rev. Evans Kisekka, bishop of Luwero Diocese; and the Rt. Rev. Onono Onweng, bishop of northern Uganda, was appointed to hear me and give its report to the archbishop.

I was scheduled to meet the committee in March 2002, but I was never summoned. "Perhaps the Church is reconsidering its stance after my appearance in the House of Bishops," I thought.

---

3. *http://www.lambethconference.org/resolutions/1998/1998-1-10.cfm.*

To my astonishment, on July 14, 2002, on the occasion of the consecration of a new bishop of Mukono Diocese, the Rt. Rev. Paul Luzinda, the dean of the province, and the Rt. Rev. Dr. Nicodemus Okille prohibited me from participating in the collective laying of hands by bishops on a new bishop on orders from the archbishop. Since I had already put on my robes, I requested that I join the procession of bishops into the church though, as directed, I would not lay my hands on the new bishop. My request was granted and I refrained from laying hands on the new bishop.

Less than two weeks after the ceremony, I received the following letter from the archbishop:

The Church of Province of Uganda
Willis Road, Namirembe
P.O. Box 14123
Kampala Uganda

July 25, 2002

The Rt. Rev. Christopher Senyonjo
Bukoto-Kyaddondo

Dear Bishop Senyonjo,

Re: Participation in church services / functions

Christian greetings and best wishes in the name of our Lord and savior Jesus Christ. As you may recall, the bishops sent the Dean of the Province to talk to you to refrain from joining the processing, vesting and laying of hands to any of Church of Uganda bishops being consecrated.

The purpose of this letter, therefore, is to confirm the bishops' stance on this issue until such a time when their difference with you is resolved.

Wishing you well.

Sincerely,
The Most Rev. Livingston Nkoyoyo
Archbishop of Church of Uganda

cc: Province Secretary of Bishops

The Church of Uganda essentially disassociated itself from me. The Most Rev. Henry Luke Orombi, Archbishop Nkoyoyo's successor, seized the opportunity to officially declare my banishment from the Church of Uganda, when on March 14, 2006, the Charismatic Church of Uganda invited me to participate in consecration of its bishop. The archbishop sent me the following correspondence:

The Church of The Province of Uganda
Willis Road, Namirembe
P.O. Box 14123, Kampala, Uganda

24th March, 2006

Christopher Ssenyonjo[4]
Bukoto
Kampala

Re: Abandonment of the Church of Uganda

According to an article in the 15th March 2006 issue of *The New Vision* you have formed a new denomination in Uganda known as the Charismatic Church of Uganda and consecrated Christopher Lwanga Tusuubira as a bishop. The article claims that the authority to do this came from your "Archbishop called Howard in America."

Pursuant to Canon 3:24.2(a)(i) of the Provincial Canons of the Church Province of Uganda (1997), we presume that you have abandoned the exercise of the ministry to which you were ordained in the Church of Uganda by this formal admission to another religious body not in communion with the Church of

---

4. This is new orthography spelling which has been mistakenly used in disregard of the official spelling of my name since my birth and even through school.

Uganda. By your action, we accept your decision to formally leave and disaffiliate from the Church of Uganda.

I have appealed to all the bishops in the Church of Uganda, active and retired, and all clergy and lay readers in the Church of Uganda, active and retired, and all Heads of Laity and wardens of the subparishes, parishes, Archdeaconries, and Diocese to uphold and enforce this decision.

You are hereby denied the right to exercise the office of a bishop or retired bishop in the Church of Uganda, including the spiritual authority as a minister of the Word and Sacraments conferred in your various ordinations.

- You are no longer entitled to wear the robes of a deacon, priest, or bishop in the Church of Uganda.
- You are no longer entitled to use the title Bishop Ssenyonjo, as if you were still a bishop in the Church of Uganda.
- You are no longer entitled to preach, speak or greet congregations in the Church of Uganda.
- You are no longer entitled to preside at weddings, funerals, baptisms, confirmations, ordinations, or Holy Communion in the Church of Uganda.
- You are no longer entitled to pronounce the absolution of sin or the blessing of God Almighty in the congregations of the Church of Uganda.
- You are no longer entitled to participate in the consecrations of bishops in the Church of Uganda.
- You are no longer entitled to participate in any liturgical celebration or function of the Church of Uganda.
- You are no longer entitled to represent the church of Uganda locally, nationally, or internationally.

Furthermore, we have advised all civil authorities in the Republic of Uganda that any license held by you for which your ordination and/or consecration in the Church of the Province of

Uganda was an indispensable qualification shall now be null and void (Canon 3:24.2(b)(ii)(2)). You have the right to appeal this decision (Canon 3:24.2(b)(i)) within six months of the date of this letter. Your appeal must contain either a statutory declaration that the facts alleged in this letter are untrue, or a retraction of the consecration of Christopher Lwanga Tusuubira as Bishop and your acknowledgement of "Archbishop called Howard" as your Archbishop.

Yours, in Christ
The Most Rev. Henry Luke Orombi
Archbishop of Church of Uganda.

The Honourable Ezekiel Muhanguzi
Provincial Chancellor

cc: All Bishops of the Church of Uganda, active and retired
All Diocesan Secretaries of the Church of Uganda
The Hon. Prime Minister of the Republic of Uganda
The Hon. Second Deputy Prime Minister/Minister of Internal Affairs
Permanent Secretary, Ministry of Internal Affairs
His Eminence, Emmanuel Cardinal Wamala
His Eminence, Metropolitan Jonah Lwanga
General Secretary, Uganda Joint Christian Council

In normal circumstances, I could have consulted church officials before performing a consecration in another church, but I could not consult Church of Uganda authorities, who had already disassociated themselves from me. During my tenure as bishop of West Buganda diocese, I was invited by the Lutheran Church in Bukoba, Tanzania, to participate in consecrating one of their bishops. On that occasion, I was not reprimanded by the Church of Uganda when I participated in that non-Anglican consecration. Moreover, the accusation that I had abandoned the Church of Uganda was false.

Despite the animosity of my former colleagues, I could not terminate my membership in the church of my birth and one which I had served as bishop for twenty-four years. I also believed that God is love and that God would not condone my discriminating against fellow believers in Christ. Therefore, nothing could prevent me from participating in a church service, of whatever denomination, when invited.

Following the controversy, the Charismatic Church of Uganda issued the following press release:

MONITOR NEWS PAPER
25/03/2006

CHARISMATIC CHURCH OF UGANDA
PRESS RELEASE

The **Rt. Rev. Dr. Christopher Disan Senyonjo (Bishop Emeritus,** West Buganda Diocese and retired Anglican Bishop) is not the owner or founder of the Charismatic Church of Uganda. Like the **Rt. Rev. Nathan Muwombi** (retired Anglican Bishop of North Mbale Diocese) and the **Rt. Rev. Hannington Bahemuka** (presiding Bishop of the Charismatic Episcopal Church, Mountain of the Moon Diocese), The **Rt. Rev. Dr. C. Senyonjo** only participated in the consecration and enthronement service of the very **Rev. Christopher Lwanga Tusubira** as Bishop of the Charismatic Church of Uganda. (By law, a priest can only become a Bishop if consecrated by not less than three Episcopal Bishops.)

After the house of Clergy of the Charismatic Church of Uganda elected the Very **Rev. C. Lwanga Tusubira** to be their Bishop, three or more Episcopal Bishops were required to consecrate him. Many retired and Presiding Bishops were approached. The three above named Bishops accepted to participate in the consecration.

The general public is hereby informed that the **Rt. Rev. Christopher Lwanga Tusubira** is the Head of the Charismatic Church of Uganda and one of the founders of this Church which started in March 2002, and was registered in August 2004.

Today, the Charismatic Church has branches in **Mbale, Kampala, Wamala, Masaka and Mityana.** Its five year programme (2005–2009) is code named **"Years of Outreach and Construction."**

The presence of The **Rt. Rev. Dr. C. Senyonjo** at the consecration and enthronement service does not in any way connect the Charismatic Church of Uganda with homosexuality or homosexuals. The church does not in any way support, advocate for or promote homosexuality.

The Church has clear objectives, doctrine and canons which are available to the general public from our head offices at **Wamala** near **Nansana** or from any of our Priests. The Charismatic Church of Uganda believes that homosexuals should be preached to, counseled and prayed for—God who changes hearts of men can change these people, and receive Jesus Christ as their personal Lord and Savior (2 Cor. 5:17)

Bishop Dr. C. Senyonjo is free, like any other Ugandan, to join our Church provided he accepts its doctrines and canons.

This statement has been issued by the Chancellor, Charismatic Church of Uganda.

I subsequently responded to the archbishop's banishment letter, in the correspondence below:

27 March 2006

The Most Rev. Henry Luke Orombi
Archbishop of Church of Uganda
P.O. Box 14123
Kampala, Uganda

The Hon. Ezekiel Muhanguzi
Provincial Chancellor
Church of Uganda

Dear Archbishop Orombi,

Re: Abandonement of The Church of Uganda

Reference is made to yours dated 24th March 2006 on the above mentioned subject:

Let it be known that I have never formed a new denomination in Uganda known as the Charismatic Church of Uganda. I am still a member of the Anglican Church of Uganda; my home church is St. Andrews church of Uganda, Bukoto. It is therefore wrong when you write in your letter that "we accept your decision to formally leave and disaffiliate from the Church of Uganda."

In light of the above it is not right for you to appeal to all bishops in the Church of Uganda, the clergy, lay leaders, heads of laity, etc. to uphold and enforce a decision which I have never made. I have never decided to abandon the Church of Uganda that I served as a Diocesan Bishop for 24 years and where I am still an active member.

My connection with the Charismatic Church of Uganda is simply to provide them with services when I am invited to do so. I believe, as a servant of Jesus Christ, that I am duty-bound to offer my services in any church founded on true Christian principles when invited. We are all one body in Christ. As such when I was approached by some of the leaders of the Charismatic Church of Uganda, I asked about the principles upon which the church was set up and whether it is legally established in Uganda. I was made to understand that it is Episcopal according to their setup and legally established in Uganda. I then agreed to be of service when invited to do so.

I was later on informed that the Church decided to consecrate one of the clergy as Bishop of the Charismatic Church of Uganda. He was introduced as the Very Rev. Christopher Tusubira Lwanga. I was impressed with him as a good choice. I was also asked to offer advice and assist in his consecration. Three Bishops participated in the consecration of Bishop Christopher Lwanga on 12 March 2006.

In your letter you mentioned a certain Archbishop Howard whom you said authorized the consecration of Bishop Christopher Lwanga. As far as I am concerned, I don't know who Archbishop Howard is. He has never exercised authority over me as an Archbishop. I have never taken any order from him.

As for exercising the office of the Bishop in the Church of Uganda, I would like to remind you, Your Grace, that your office had already stopped me from doing any church service since 14 July 2002, when we were consecrating the Bishop of Mukono Diocese. The incident at Mukono was (retroactively) enforced by the letter of the Archbishop on 25 July 2002.

Your Grace, all these years I have been neglected and have not been allowed to practice my rightful role as bishop. I am therefore grateful to the Charismatic Church of Uganda, which allowed me to serve whenever they invite me.

Your Grace, I would like to categorically inform you that I am entitled to using the title Bishop, even when the church leadership chooses not to recognize me as Bishop in the Church of Uganda. The title of Bishop is not sacrosanct to the Anglican Church of Uganda alone. I was consecrated in the Church of God. I belong to the church in the royal priesthood of all believers, 1 Peter 2:9.

As regards the nullification of any indispensable qualification I hold, as per your second last paragraph advising the civil authority in the republic of Uganda, let it be clear to all, that whatever I hold is by my right as a rightful citizen of Uganda, and not because I am a Bishop.

Furthermore, as I listened to your press conference, you said something about human sexuality. Your Grace, as you may be aware, I have been insisting all along that we in the Church, as recommended in the Lambeth Conference 1998, should discuss biblical teachings about this matter, to be able to handle the emerging issues within the church.

I would like to conclude my letter to you by saying something about my counseling services. Since 1998, I have been engaged in counseling all persons without discrimination. People with different issues contact me, and as a counselor I have to make it absolutely clear that I should not condemn, but be empathetic and guide people. All people are welcome, especially the depressed, rejected, abused, and the minority in our communities— Luke 4:18–19.

I hope the above will clear the false accusations framed against me.

Yours in Christ,
The Rt. Rev. Bishop Dr. D. Christopher Senyonjo

c.c. All Bishops of the Church of Uganda, active and retired
c.c. All Diocesan Secretaries of the Church of Uganda
c.c. The Hon. Prime Minister of the Republic of Uganda
c.c The Hon. Second Deputy Prime Minister / Minister of Internal Affairs
c.c. Permanent Secretary, Ministry of Internal Affairs
c.c. His Eminence, Emmanuel Cardinal Wamala
c.c. His Eminence, Metropolitan Jonah Lwanga
c.c. General Secretary, Uganda Joint Christian Council

Neither the archbishop nor the provincial chancellor responded to this letter. Instead, the archbishop waited long after the expiration of stipulated time for me to appeal, and then wrote me the following letter:

The Church of the Province of Uganda
Willis Road, Namirembe
P.o. Box 14123, Kampala, Uganda

16th January 2007

Christopher SsenyonjoBukoto
Kampala

Re: Notice of Abandonment of the Exercise of the Ministry

Dear Christopher,

On 24th March 2006 I wrote you a letter, which you, Bishop Okille, and I also discussed in my office that day. Because of your unauthorized consecration of Christopher Lwanga Tusuubira as a Bishop in the Charismatic Church of Uganda, we informed you that, pursuant to Canon 3:24.2(a) (i) of the Provincial Canons of the Church of the Province of Uganda (1997), we presume that you have abandoned the exercise of the ministry to which you were ordained in the Church of Uganda. By your action we accepted your decision to formally leave and disaffiliate from the Church of Uganda.

We also informed you that you have the right to appeal this decision (Canon 3:24.2(b) (i)) within six months of the date of the letter. That six-month period concluded on 25th September 2006. We never received an appeal from you during that time, nor have we received an appeal from you in the additional months since then, given as a grace period.

It has always been my sincere desire that you would repent of your actions and make an appeal in writing. In the absence, however, of such an appeal which needed to contain either a statutory declaration that the facts alleged in my letter of 24th March 2006 were untrue, or a retraction of the consecration of Christopher Lwanga Tusuubira as Bishop, we hereby declare formally that you have abandoned the Church of Uganda, and we no longer consider you to be a Bishop of the Church of Uganda.

Accordingly, as the Canons stipulate in Schedule D, "This is a notification that Christopher Senyonjo, having been admitted to the office of Bishop in the Church of the Province of Uganda, has abandoned the exercise of that ministry according to the terms of Canon 3.24 of the Provincial Assembly of the Church of the Province of Uganda."

You will always be remembered historically as the second Bishop of West Buganda Diocese, but you are no longer a retired Bishop of the Church of Uganda and are no longer entitled to the rights and privileges of that status.

Yours, in Christ,
The Most Rev. Henry Luke Orombi
Archbishop of the Church of Uganda

The Honorable Ezekiel Muhanguzi
Provincial Chancellor

cc: All Bishops of the Church of Uganda
Provincial Secretary
All Heads of Departments, Provincial Secretariat
All clergy and lay leaders of West Buganda and Kampala Dioceses

My response to the archbishop's letter follows.

Bishop Christopher Senyonjo
P.O. Box 7296
Kampala (U)

Date: 6th March 2007

The Most Rev. Henry Luke Orombi
Archbishop of Church of Uganda
P.o. Box 14123, Kampala (U)

The Hon. Ezekiel Muhanguzi
Provincial Chancellor
Church of Uganda

Dear Archbishop Orombi,

Ref: Response To the Notice of Abandonment of Exercise of the
Ministry

Thank you for your letter dated 16th January 2007 that I received
on 23rd February 2007. I hope in future the letters addressed to
me should clearly identify me. I am a graduate with a doctorate
degree. So it is not proper to simply write Christopher Senyonjo
on the envelope, as if I am a small boy.

I am a Bishop in the Church of God even if you no longer want to recognize me as such in the Church of Uganda. Theologically, there is one Baptism, one confirmation, one ordination to deaconate, priesthood, and episcopate. These you cannot undo by a stroke of a pen.

It is my prayer that the Holy Spirit guides and reminds you of what we discussed in your office as regards the letter of 24th March 2006. I told you that I have not and I will never "decide to formally leave and disaffiliate from the Church of Uganda." This is also clearly stated in my letter to you of 27 March 2006 in paragraph 1 and 2. Your Grace should know it once for all that I am still an active member of the Church of Uganda which I served as a Diocesan Bishop for 24 years.

I am amazed, though painfully wondering about what is going on in our church, it is very wrong when you state that you never received any appeal or response from me since 24th March 2006. I categorically state that I responded to your letter of 24th March 2006, in my letter to you of 27th March 2006, barely three days after receiving yours. I personally delivered that letter to your office at Namirembe and handed it to your white personal secretary. . . .

Again it defeats my understanding when you state that "it has always been my sincere desire that you would repent of your actions and make an appeal in writing." An appeal of which you dictate what must be contained therein. Repentance is self-accusation, conviction and evaluation. However, in my letter to you of 27th March 2006, it is clearly shown that you wrongly accused me; and to put in your own words, "the facts alleged in your letter of 24th March 2006 were untrue," see the attached copy of 27th March 2006 in paragraph 1 and 2 and the last sentence of the letter.

As to the fact of retracting the consecration of Christopher Tusuubira Lwanga as Bishop, I cannot be so hypocritical that far, as some of the highly placed clergy do, to the extent of usurping the powers of the Holy Spirit. **Once ordained by God no man can retract.**

It is my prayer and request that you retract the notification you have stated, because you are wrong in saying, "has abandoned the exercise of the ministry." If you cannot, then state that **you are forcing me to abandon the exercise of the ministry.**

As a reminder, your Grace, I historically have been the third Bishop of West Buganda Diocese and not the second as you stated.

If I was admitted in the office of the Bishop of the Province of Uganda, and I am no longer a retired Bishop, then what am I?

As for the entitlement of the rights and privileges of the status, you have wrongly denied me that, since 25th July 2002.

Since I never abandoned the calling in the Church of Uganda, I should be accorded all the rights as a retired Bishop since 1998.

I conclude by St. Paul's words: "The letter kills but the spirit gives life" (2 Cor. 3:6).

The Rt. Rev. Bishop D. Christopher Senyonjo DD; DMin
Retired Bishop of West Buganda Diocese

Copy:
All Bishop of the Church of Uganda
Provincial Secretary
All Heads of Departments, Provincial Secretary
All Clergy and Lay leader of West Buganda and Kampala Dioceses

The archbishop never responded to this letter either. I sought an audience with him by appointment several times without success. I was very disappointed when he retired without granting me a meeting. I am still a loyal member of the church, and I have not disobeyed the order of the church banning me from baptizing, confirming, or officiating sacraments in the Anglican Church of Uganda.

I was greatly distressed recently when I could not officiate at a wedding of a son of one of the couples whom I married forty years earlier. When the young man requested that I officiate at his marriage ceremony, I was saddened to tell him that the Church of Uganda had prohibited me from performing such ceremonies. I advised him to find another person to conduct the ceremony as it was unlikely that the church would grant me a special dispensation to officiate at his wedding.

Many Christians are perplexed and surprised about the church's punitive actions against me. They never imagined such politics in the church. Some have publicly expressed support for my stance.[5]

The Church of Uganda was not alone in its prejudice against LGBTQ persons. In the recent past, Uganda's Parliament joined the antigay hysteria by introducing and passing a frightening anti-LGBTQ bill with the moral support of external antigay groups.

In March 2009, I attended a conference in Uganda titled "Exposing the Truth behind Homosexuality and the Homosexual Agenda." Some of the main speakers included activist Dr. Scott Lively; Mr. Don Schmierer, executive of Exodus International; and Mr. Caleb Lee Brundidge, of the International Healing Foundation. Dr. Lively's presentation fired up the attendees, which included members of Parliament and government officials. I believe Mr. Lively planted the seed for Uganda's Antihomosexuality bill on that day.

Some of the highlights of Mr. Lively's presentation included:

"Most of the people . . . they say gays are born that way and it has been . . . proven. . . . That is a lie. That's what's called a lie. It is not true. There is no definitive scientific study that has ever proved that homosexuality is innate."

"If homosexuality is not caused by genetic factors . . . then that means it can be acquired. . . . **And if it can be acquired, shouldn't we be doing everything in our power to protect people from acquiring it?** Shouldn't we lean to the side of protecting

---

5. I refer you to a touching e-mail in appendix 1a by Mr. Mayanja Kizito John addressed to the archbishop on April 3, 2006, in support of my work.

the children instead of affirming a scientific hypothesis that has no actual truthful foundation?"

"If someone is identifying themselves based on their orientation toward a person of the same gender, then that seems to me to be a **self-evident disorder**."

"If you catch them at 12 years old, which they are working very aggressively to do and you tell those children that if you have an attraction towards someone of the same gender, that means you're gay and because you're gay you need to come with us."

"There's a whole network of people ready to simply inculcate you and enfold you into their world and they want more and more people in their world because they are in a campaign to change everything."

"[Homosexuality and pedophilia] they are equated. They are equated because the very same arguments you can make for homosexuality you can apply to pedophilia in many ways, not in every way but in many ways. . . . Clearly it's not the way it ought to be. It's wrong and it should be discouraged."

"Even though probably the majority of homosexuals are not oriented towards young people, there is a significant number that are, especially the men. . . . Male homosexuality has historically been not adult to adult it has been adult to teenager."

"The gay movement is an evil institution [whose] goal is to defeat the marriage-based society and replace it with a culture of sexual promiscuity in which there's no restrictions on sexual conduct except the principle of mutual choice."

"We divide those between the person that we love and the movement that we hate."

"The gay movement doesn't care about what you think . . . they're focused on the young ones because if you can put the ideas into their minds it's just a matter of time before you die off and they take your place and their value system will then allow all the rules to be changed."

"There is a norm; there is a model of the way things are supposed to be. When you find yourself outside of that, when you find yourself not fitting the way things are designed to be, it's a simple matter of just learning how you ought to be and working to restore the way things are supposed to be."

". . . Dealing with these sexual disorders, you ask 'what is it supposed to look like?' 'What's the norm?' The norm is the heterosexual design of the body."

"The marriage-based society . . . discourages all the competing alternatives to marriage. You can't have a marriage-based society and a social value of sexual freedom. They don't work together."

"The real danger of the gay movement is its necessary goal of the elimination of this moral system in order to achieve this [sexual freedom]."

"**. . . That is the gay agenda. . . . It is the recreation of society on a different moral foundation and the problem with that is that moral foundation will lead to social chaos and destruction.**"

"We've seen the transformation of America, when at the pinnacle of its Christianity was probably in the 1950s. Ever since then it has been declining, why? Because of the sexual revolution. Where did the sexual revolution come from? The sexual revolution came from the activists of the American gay movement."

"There is no other group of sinners in the world that is organized for the purpose of transforming the society in its own image."

"Nobody has been able to stop them [homosexuals] so far, I'm hoping Uganda can."[6]

One month after the conference, a member of Uganda's Parliament introduced the "Anti-Homosexuality Bill of 2009." It proposed, among other things, a death penalty for "aggravated homosexuality," and mandated jail terms for people who do not report homosexuals in their midst and for those who "promote homosexuality." Following

---

6. *http://www.publiceye.org/publications/globalizing-the-culture-wars/scott-lively-quotes.php.* Emphasis in the original.

unrelenting international criticism, the Parliament dropped the death penalty provision in favor of life in prison.

In March 2010, the Rev. Canon Byamugisha, Major Rubaramira, Mr. Frank Mugisha, Ms. Florence Baluba, and I presented a petition to the speaker of Parliament urging the withdrawal of the bill. On December 20, 2013, Parliament passed the bill. On February 14, the president signed the bill into law and the act became law on March 10, 2014.

In April 2014, the Civil Society Coalition on Human Rights & Constitutional Law released a press statement challenging the law:

PRESS STATEMENT
FOR IMMEDIATE RELEASE

Friday 25th April 2014,

UGANDA'S ANTI-HOMOSEXUALITY ACT CHALLENGED BEFORE THE EAST AFRICAN COURT OF JUSTICE

(KAMPALA) Represented by the Human Rights Awareness and Promotion Forum (HRAPF)[7], the Civil Society Coalition on Human Rights and Constitutional Law (CSCHRCL) on 23rd April 2014 filed a reference before the East African Court of Justice contending that Uganda is in violation of the Treaty for the Establishment of the East African Community by enacting the Anti-Homosexuality Act 2014, certain provisions of which are inconsistent with the obligations laid down by the treaty. HRAPF is a human rights organization working to achieve equality, non-discrimination and equal access to justice for marginalized groups in Uganda.

The reference argues that certain provisions of Uganda's Anti-Homosexuality Act, Act 4 of 2014 are in violation of the Treaty for the Establishment of the East African Community in Articles 6(d), 7(2) and 8(1) (c) which enjoins partner states to govern their

7. HRAPF is a human rights organization that advocates, and provides legal assistance, for marginalized groups in Uganda.

populace according to the principles of good governance, democracy, the Rule of Law, social justice and the maintenance of universally accepted standards of human rights which include inter alia, provision of equal opportunities and gender equality as well as the recognition, promotion and protection of human and people's rights in accordance with the provisions of the African Charter on Human and People's Rights.

According to the HRAPF Executive Director, Adrian Jjuuko, "Since the Act became law on 10th March 2014, human rights violations against LGBTI persons have been recorded including arrests, cases of mob justice, and raids on offices, all of which violate the human rights guaranteed in the African Charter on Human and People's Rights and other international instruments. This goes against the obligations imposed upon partner states of the East African Community to maintain universally-accepted standards of human rights."

"The filing of this reference is part of the CSCHRCL's commitment to use all the available legal avenues in order to ensure that human rights and the rule of law are respected in Uganda. The East African Court of Justice is one of the avenues that we are using, and we hope that the Court finds in our favour," stated Geoffrey Ogwaro, Co-Coordinator of the Civil Society Coalition.

The Applicant has asked the East African Court of Justice to make declarations to the effect that certain provisions of the Anti-Homosexuality Act, 2014 violate the principles that partner states are enjoined to follow under the Treaty for the Establishment of the East African Court of Justice.[8]

In August 2014, the Constitutional Court ruled the law invalid. Nonetheless, the Parliament is currently plotting to reintroduce it.

In October 2010, the atmosphere surrounding the LGBTQ debate became extremely poisonous when a local tabloid called

---

8. The Office of the Civil Society Coalition on Human Rights and Constituional law.

Rolling Stone published photos of what it referred to as the "100 top homosexuals" in Uganda. Even though I am heterosexual, my photograph was on the front page along with David Kato's and others'. The headline read, "Hang them"![9]

On the basis of privacy and safety concerns, David Kato, one of the pioneer LGBTQ rights activists in Uganda, sued the paper to compel it to stop publishing the photos and names of those it presumed to be homosexuals. The court ruled in his favor. In January 2011, David was murdered under unclear circumstances.

David's local priest refused to officiate at his funeral. Instead, he sent a lay reader to officiate on his behalf. At the funeral, the lay reader went on a tirade against LGBTQ persons, telling them to repent lest they go to hell. Overwhelmed by emotion and anger, Kasha, one of the prominent LGBTQ activists in Uganda, pulled the microphone away from the lay reader. In the ensuing commotion, mourners rushed David's casket to the gravesite. I was present, but I was not officiating due to the Church of Uganda's proscription of my services. Following the abrupt turn of events, I was moved by the Holy Spirit to intervene—I loudly called for calm. Surprised by my intervention, the mourners, thankfully, listened.

I told them that the David I knew was a good human being and a great human rights activist and that we should thank God for his service to humanity. Further, I told them that it was not right to pass judgment against anyone, as heaven was for all believers: straight, gay, or other. I prayed for David's soul. I was happy to facilitate granting him a dignified Christian burial.[10]

---

9. This headline is eerily similar to Idi Amin's soldiers' earlier refrain of "Kill them" in regard to the bishops shortly before Archbishop Luwum was murdered.

10. David's story, LGBTQ activism in Uganda, and my participation in his burial are documented in a film titled *Call Me Kuchu*, which was shown in various cities around the United States. Another film that touches on LGBTQ rights in Uganda titled *God Loves Uganda* was released later.

St. Paul's Reconciliation and Equality Centre

Despite all the animosity, I thank God who has enabled me to continue counseling and giving spiritual hope to LGBTQ persons and other marginalized people in Uganda through St. Paul's Reconciliation and Equality Centre (SPREC) that I founded in 2010. At SPREC we endeavor to provide LGBTQ persons access to medical care and economic empowerment in the face of discrimination. I am grateful to all those who have facilitated this work through their time, donations, and encouragement. I am particularly grateful to music legend Elton John, who generously funded SPREC's HIV/AIDS outreach for two years.

As a bishop, I believe that I am called to bring straight and LGBTQ people together in the true spirit of Christianity, bearing love, compassion, and understanding. What is needed is conversation and understanding in the spirit of compassion. Draconian laws are destructive and are against humanity itself when they aim to eliminate marginalized people who should instead be protected by law. Therefore, the broader mission of St. Paul's Reconciliation and Equality Centre is to foster programs and activities that alleviate the suffering, discrimination, and injustices that women, the poor, and marginalized communities face within Uganda.

The LGBTQ Debate

In the course of my ministry to LGBTQ persons, I have engaged in conversations with people opposed to my ministry to LGBTQ persons. These individuals invariably cite the Bible (religious edicts) and culture as bases for their abhorrence of LGBTQ sexuality and orientation.

They consistently argue that God did not intend for same sex unions, creating Adam and Eve to be complementary to each other. Moreover, God commanded us to go forth and multiply; homosexuality, on the other hand, is nonreproductive. My response is that God's ways are beyond human understanding. His creation has a variety of characteristics, for instance: omnivorous and carnivorous; poisonous and benign; left-handed and right-handed; barren and fertile; dark-skinned (like me) and light-skinned; and even hermaphrodites and the rest of us. Given this variance, who are we to judge God's creation?

In regards to sexuality, I explain that all of us—straight, gay, lesbian, or transgender—inherited human weakness deriving from the original sin when Adam gave into temptation. Sharing the forbidden fruit in the Garden of Eden was a gesture of intimacy between Adam and Eve; moreover, eating it gave them pleasure. In this regard, romantic relationships (straight or LGBTQ) are essentially an expression of the inherent human need for intimacy, sharing, and pleasure; all sentiments which transcend the need to procreate.

The biblical story of Sodom and Gomorrah (Genesis 19) is often misused to justify Christians' antihomosexual views. There are two points to note here: First, a close reading of the story indicates that it only condemned the depraved use of homosexuality to humiliate strangers, but not homosexuals, per se. In Ezekiel 16:49, we read that the sin of Sodom was the lack of hospitality, although Sodom was blessed with affluence. And second, there is no reference anywhere in the gospel of Jesus condemning homosexuals, even though the story of Sodom and Gomorrah predated him.

And while LGBTQ individuals may not have biological children, many do in fact love children and are capable of adopting and nurturing them. Indeed, in the United States, loving LGBTQ couples can adopt children, including those abandoned by heterosexual parents.

On the other hand, cultural relativists such as Pastor Sempa in Uganda argue that not only is homosexuality against biblical edicts, it is also a foreign practice contrary to their African culture. I find cultural arguments particularly tenuous. First, in the case of homosexuals, cultural arguments discount their inherent nature: many LGBTQ individuals recount feeling different from peers of the same sex; even as children they sensed their sexual inclinations. Second, cultural arguments have historically been used to subjugate minorities, women, and children. In many African cultures, for example, it is still not customary for women to own land. And not too long ago, it was a cultural taboo for women to eat chicken in Buganda.[11] Third, historical evidence shows that homosexuality is in fact not foreign—it has long existed in African societies. A case in point is a recent book about an Ethiopian woman, Walatta Petros (1592–1642), a saint in Ethiopia's ancient Christian church who was reportedly in a long-term same-sex relationship with a fellow nun.[12] Her story is particularly instructive because Ethiopia was never colonized.

Finally, culture is not static; it adapts and changes as society gets more enlightenment through education, science, and exposure.

Currently LGBTQ sexuality seems foreign to many in Uganda since LGBTQ persons often live incognito due to fear and intimidation. But in due time Ugandans shall recognize them as different but normal human beings who have a right to consensual adult relationships with people whom they love. This realization is bound to occur once the diversity of human sexuality is universally broached in educational institutions.[13]

Ugandan LGBTQ Voices

I am honored that Felix, Drew, Tau, Melissa, Rodney, Kati, and Jeff (not their actual names) are willing to share their experience of LGBTQ life in Uganda.[14] With the exception of Felix's story, which I narrate, the rest are first-person accounts.

---

11. Chicken, which was considered a delicacy, was reserved for men!

12. *The Life and Struggles of Our Mother Walatta Petros: A Seventeenth-Century African Biography of an Ethiopian Woman*, by Galawdewos, translated and edited by Laura Belcher and Michael Kleiner (Princeton, NJ: Princeton University Press, 2015).

13. Hetero- or homosexual relations are only wrong when they are nonconsensual, as in rape, defilement, incest, or bestiality, not in the case of consenting adults.

14. They each expressly gave me permission to share their stories.

Felix

Felix is a chef in his midtwenties. Two of his younger siblings, a brother and a sister, are married. When he came of age, Felix's family urged him to marry but, whenever his mother broached the subject, he evaded her. Many beautiful girls were introduced to Felix, but he showed them no interest.

Worried about him, Felix's mother asked a local pastor to speak to him. Felix confided in the pastor that he had no interest in girls; rather, he told the pastor that he was attracted to men. Taken aback, the pastor advised Felix to pray to God to change his disposition.

After weeks of prayer, Felix felt no change. The pastor instructed him to pray even harder and to fast for thirty days. Felix prayed and fasted as directed, but nothing changed. The pastor told Felix that God would reject him if he did not change—he would be rendered a lost soul.

Felix was extremely troubled; he gave up on God and despaired on life itself. But, by God's providence, he sought my counseling services. On listening to him, I advised Felix to accept himself as God created him. Felix was so relieved by the good news that he decided to tell his mother who he really was.

When Felix told his mother that he was gay, she broke into tears; he cried along with her. After sobbing, the mother said to him: "Felix, you are my son despite being different from your siblings." Felix embraced his mother in jubilation for he had not expected this reaction. He felt elated because his mother had finally accepted him for whom he was. Two months following this rapprochement, the mother passed away. But Felix was grateful that she died after reconciling with him.

I am grateful that Felix allowed me to open this chapter with his story. Now one of my closest confidants, he often tells me that he may have committed suicide without the counsel I provided to him.

DREW

I am currently in Senior Four[15] vacation. It is by God's grace that I have reached this far because during the course of my secondary school studies, I have been expelled from a couple of schools due to my views on homosexuality. In the first instance, when I expressed my views on homosexuality in a dormitory discussion one day, my dorm mates reported me to the school's administration. The administrators informed my parents that they were expelling me from the school to prevent me from teaching other students deviant views and bad behaviors.

On reaching home, my father interrogated me, but calmed down when I convinced him that it was merely a discussion. But when my stepmother, with whom I stayed, heard the reason for my expulsion, she told me that I could no longer stay with her. I relocated to my father's second wife's home and joined another school. But I was expelled again when a teacher from my former school who worked part-time in my new school saw me and reported me to school authorities.

I am grateful that my father did not give up on my education, but I am very confused. I cannot tell him the truth due to the prevailing negative attitudes in Uganda about homosexuality. I am depressed and I feel hopeless, voiceless. I do not know what the future holds for me.

TAU

I am twenty-two years old, and I am on course to receive a certificate in primary education, but I feel like I am at the crossroads with nowhere to go.

At all Christian churches that I have attended, preachers curse homosexuals of whom I am. I have tried to change, but without

---

15. Secondary school, grade 11, after which a student joins senior secondary school (A-level), on passing O-level exams.

success. I am wondering why I was created a homosexual. I hate myself; I do not know where I belong.

Once, when I brought up rights of homosexuals in a youth committee of which I was a member, I was shut down and expelled. When the remaining committee members informed my parents of the reason for my expulsion, my parents declared that I would bring them shame and isolation from the community. I tried to explain my feelings to them, but they would not listen. Instead, my parents expelled me from home. I am now alone. I feel cursed and neglected.

I no longer talk about my sexuality; I fear that people may harm and even kill me. I feel insecure.

I ask the Almighty God for protection.

Melissa

I am a teenager in a girl's secondary school. My parents often buy me dresses and skirts, but I don't like dressing like girls, because I don't feel like a girl. I identify with boys and I prefer boys' clothes. But I am afraid of telling the truth because I don't want to drop out of school.

One day, I asked my parents to buy for me trousers similar to ones I saw other girls wear. In response, they told me that the church condemns females who dress like men. And that if I wanted to dress like men, they rather I looked for another home.

I am confused and stressed. I no longer feel confident because I am living a lie. And I cannot express my feelings. It is psychological torture; I feel as if I am in a prison.

I pray that God grants me the patience and tolerance to enable me to complete my studies. My vow to God is that I will advocate for human rights and freedom of speech once I finish my studies. For I don't wish my experience on any other person.

Rodney

When I was twenty years old, my father suggested that I get married—I was not interested, but I urged him to wait until I finished my studies.

When I turned twenty-four, my father summoned clan leaders to talk to me, for he wanted me to get married but was worried because neither he nor other family members had ever seen me with a girl. Indeed, I had only male friends. I told the clan leaders that I shall marry in due time. Disappointed, my family accused my friend of being a bad influence on me and banned him from ever setting foot in our home again.

At twenty-six, my father summoned me to the living room to tell me that he had found a girl for me to marry—he was aging and as his only son he wished that I extended the family's lineage.[16]At that very moment, I decided to tell him the truth: I told him that I was gay.

My father threatened to curse and disown me—I gave in and got married. I am now thirty-two years old, but my marriage is unstable because I do not love my wife. I don't know what to do. And since I lost my friend, I have not had any peace of mind.

I hate myself and my family; life is too complicated.

KATI

I am a twenty-nine-year old man with a degree in business administration. For the past five years, my family has been pressuring me to get married. They say that I am getting old; it is time I settled down. They have introduced several girls to me, but I have told them that I am not interested in marriage. Due to my refusal to marry, my father expelled me from home.

When I rented a house in a trading center, my father dissuaded the landlord from renting to me and I got evicted. Whenever I apply for a job, I lose it on account of my relatives tarnishing my name. They say that I am an antisocial, dangerous person. In desperation, I have reverted to witchcraft to help me procure potions to protect me and to help me secure a job.

---

16. In our culture, the family lineage (and the clan's) is solely traced through males.

Some individuals recently stoned my house, and banged on the doors and windows. They screamed that I should leave the community: I was a bad influence on their children whom they did not want me to turn into homosexuals. When I reported the incident to the police, they simply advised me to relocate to another area.

I am perplexed because I have done no wrong to anyone, but I am being harassed. I do not feel safe anywhere. My family hates me and I cannot get a job. I do not know what to do.

JEFF

I am a thirty-one-year-old man whose parents are pastors. As a child, I felt special because only I, among my siblings, was allowed to sit at the dinner table with my parents.[17] Consequently, I thought they showed me extra care and love.

At school, which I loved, I did not relate with girls. In fact, I did not enjoy associating with them. On the contrary, I felt joy when I associated with fellow boys. When I joined secondary school, my peers attributed my lack of interaction with girls to shyness, not realizing that I had no interest in girls whatsoever.

When I became an adult, I developed sexual attraction toward fellow males. But I could not tell anyone, not even my parents. The church, of which my parents were part, condemned homosexuality. Moreover, life for openly gay people was so stressful and fearful that some even committed suicide.

One day, I narrated my dilemma to a counselor: I told him that I was uncomfortable with my natural inclinations. In response, the counselor advised me to accept myself as a gay person whom God had created me that way: I could not change into something I was not.

He also assured me that God had created me in his image and loved me. This good news got me interested in theology. I joined a

17. Traditionally in Uganda, parents sat at the dinner table, separate from the children. This was perhaps due to the fact that the traditional home included many children (including extended family children) who could not all fit at the dinner table.

Bible college to learn more about God's affirming love. My reading confirmed that indeed God loves us all—gay or straight, white or black, disabled or able-bodied.

Empowered by this affirmation, I developed the courage and the strength to rejoice in who I am. I found a boyfriend with whom I stayed for more than ten years. Unfortunately, I found out later that not only was my boyfriend bisexual, he also had a wife with whom he had conceived a child!

He and I had started some small businesses together, including an Internet café, a mobile money kiosk, and a restaurant. In due time, my boyfriend's wife began to suspect that we were involved in a gay relationship. She reported us to the police just prior to the president signing an antigay bill which criminalized homosexuality in Uganda.

One inauspicious day, as my partner and I were working, some policemen came to our business premises. They forcibly took me to Kisugu police station on account of stories that I was gay. After some "investigations," they arrested me and charged me with sodomy.

To my surprise, my friend registered himself as a complainant, alleging that I had used him! I was taken to a prison. Life in prison was miserable. Policemen tortured me and for the first two days I hardly ate anything: the food was inedible. I became so weak that other inmates begged the officers to take me to a hospital. The officers did nothing—but I eventually adjusted to prison conditions and survived.

After some time, the officer-in-charge presented me a document to sign. I refused to sign the document, which I had not been given an opportunity to read. The officer pointed a gun at my head and threatened to shoot if I did not sign. Under duress, I signed.

Soon rumors circulated that I had confessed to being a homosexual. Shocked by the "confession," my friends and fellow church members stopped visiting me. It was abhorrent to them that their pastor was a homosexual! The few people, including lawyers, who still came to check on me were told that I was no longer at that location so they would leave without seeing me.

On one occasion, prison authorities took me to a doctor to ostensibly confirm whether or not I was gay: you can imagine the humiliation! Two weeks following the "test," I was given a police bond which temporarily granted me leave from prison. After a week, I was rearrested and taken to court. At court, the magistrate sentenced me to a month in prison, but I got court bail.

Upon my release, the officer in charge of criminal investigations advised me to stay away from my former neighborhood, as I could be assaulted and even killed by angry neighbors.

Indeed, I returned to a drastically different environment. My partner now claimed sole ownership of the businesses that we had started together. He even had the gall to advise me to independently start new ventures as I was still alive and able.

The church, where I had been a pastor, informed me that members had resolved that they should not employ homosexuals. Worse still, I got evicted from my house. But I could not afford to rent another place, as I did not have any money.

Homeless and penniless, I trudged up Prayer Mountain, an open space that is open to anyone without regard to race, gender, or status. Without shelter, I endured drenching rain, searing sunshine, and pesky mosquitoes. It was also cold at night. Perhaps as a result, a case of Hepatitis B which I had caught while in prison recurred. I vomited blood and passed bloody diarrhea. But I could not afford treatment and my relatives shunned me.

By God's providence, a Good Samaritan took me to hospital. But I did not finish the prescribed course of treatment due to a lack of funds. Nonetheless, I recovered with God's help.

Rather than change who I am, this unpleasant experience emboldened me. I developed the courage to fight for gay rights and freedom in Uganda. In this resolve, I was strengthened by the bible, John 16:33:

> In the world you face persecution. But take courage; I have conquered the world!

And I was spurred to action by Isaiah 61:1:

The spirit of the Lord God is upon me,
  because the Lord has anointed me;
he has sent me to bring good news to the oppressed,
  to bind up the broken-hearted,
to proclaim liberty to the captives,
  and release to the prisoners.

Persecution of homosexuals in Uganda is largely based on the false notion that we are made or influenced into homosexuality by general depravity or foreign influence. But the reality for me and for many other gay people I know is that we were born gay. In fact, I was inherently drawn to fellow males since childhood. Thus, my message to fellow homosexuals is to accept and love themselves as they are. For God created us in his own image and loves us. He will never leave us alone; we should not lose hope.

We shall overcome in due time. In the meantime let us be consoled by Isaiah 53:5: "But he was wounded for our transgressions, crushed for our iniquities; upon him was the punishment that made us whole, and by his bruises we are healed."

Let us stay strong in spirit and bear our tears today, for tomorrow we shall share laughter.

Thanks be to God.

These are just a few accounts of the LGBTQ community's experience in Uganda. They need the Good News according to Jesus Christ, but the church is precluding them from it!

Christ's Love Transcends All Prejudice and Persecution

Hostility against homosexuals is often justified through interpretations of the Bible. I believe this is wrong. Even though we may not agree on how to interpret the Bible, we should emulate Jesus, who welcomed all without discrimination. Why should we repel individuals from Christ simply because they are homosexual when Jesus did not shun them? Moreover, the Bible (John 15:12) enjoins us to love one another. Persecution is not love.

People of goodwill should nurse no ill-will, support no recrimination, nor oppression, nor discrimination against any human being. Though we may have differences in colors of our skin, shapes of our noses, and in sexual orientation, our God is one and is the God of love.

Seeking the harm of people different from us dissipates the energy that should be invested in human progress. It hinders development and prosperity, for there are talented people across the divide of our differences. Discrimination not only suffocates their talent, but also leads to untold suffering. Love is the source of bliss; and when we love, we are of God.

Moreover, it is important to note that:

- Homosexual relations are not sins in and of themselves just as heterosexual relations are not sins (or crimes) of themselves, except in cases of rape, defilement, and pedophilia.
- Homosexuals are human beings who need love and deserve the respect and due regard accorded to all human beings.
- Homosexual orientation cannot be controlled through willpower, as "conversion therapists" claim.

Recommendations to the Church

First, the Church should be inclusive:

Many homosexuals have abandoned the church, which they view as judgmental and unwelcoming. Some have returned to church when love and understanding have been extended to them. When the church rejects homosexual persons, it is like when a parent abandons a child; the child may fall in bad company.

Second, the church should listen to homosexuals, but listening and counseling should not be intended to "deprogram" homosexuals. We have neither power nor authority to alter God's creation.

Third, seminaries should introduce prerequisite courses in human sexuality, since many theologians and priests are currently not equipped to deal with human sexuality in all its variances. The words of retired Roman Catholic Bishop Thomas Gumbleton of Detroit are a case in point:

> Unfortunately, I am aware how difficult it is going to be for the church to change. How difficult it will be for bishops throughout our country to see that ordained priests have openness to the gay and lesbian community. I know it will be difficult because I can speak from personal experience. The seminary formation I received was reinforced by the culture in which I grew up. It did not prepare me in any way to minister effectively to gay and lesbian people. . . . Not very long ago my own brother, Dan, wrote a letter to our family in which he declared that he is gay. He and his partner have a very good relationship. It is humbling for me to acknowledge that I would not even deal with that letter for several months. I simply refused to respond. . . . I am very blessed that I met Olga, because she helped me to be much more accepting of my own brother and his partner. I am especially grateful because a short time before my mother died, she asked me, "What is going to happen Dan? Will he go to hell?" . . . Because I had come to know Olga and to imbibe from her something of the compassion, the love, and the pride that she felt [for her son], I was able to speak with my mother in a very understanding way; which I might not have been able to do otherwise.[18]

---

18. Thomas Gumbleton, retired auxiliary bishop of Detroit, "A Call to Listen: The Church's Pastoral and Theological Response to Gays and Lesbians," in *More than a Monologue, Volume 1: Sexual Diversity and the Catholic Church Voices of Our Time*, ed. Christine Firer Hinze and J. Patrick Hornbeck II (New York: Fordham University Press, 2014), 51–54.

Fourth, premarital counseling should fully address the question of human sexuality. I have met couples who are unhappy because they married against their natural instincts; many eventually separate. But the separation is often a very painful experience to their offspring.

Fifth, parents of homosexual children should love them without discrimination; this should be true for all our relations, kith and kin.

Sixth, we should not discriminate nor hate anybody for being different from us.

However difficult it may be for many people to understand the phenomenon of homosexual orientation, it should not be an excuse to violate the human rights of others. Homosexuals should not be excluded from the church nor should they be denied jobs and housing. Homosexuality is not a crime. Most importantly, prejudice, violence, and discrimination must not be countenanced by all morally upright people, let alone Christians.

6

Celebrations

SINCE OUR MARRIAGE ON DECEMBER 28, 1963, Mary has been a great companion to me. I consider her a precious jewel. By the grace of God's unfathomable love, Mary and I celebrated our Golden Anniversary at Namirembe Cathedral on December 28, 2013. We thanked the Lord, for it is by his grace that we both lived to see the day; we also thanked him for his many blessings to us.

God has blessed us with several children: Joseph Sebulime, Grace Nambusi, Peter Kyambadde, David Muyanja, John Yoweri Sekiwu, Faith Nanyonjo, Timothy Mbaziira, Moses Sembusi, Margaret Night Nabulime, Andrew Talemwa, and Judith Nakalyango. They are all unique, interesting individuals. The variety in their character is like a rainbow. God has also blessed us with many grandchildren.

During the fifty years of our marriage, Mary and I endured many trying moments. In addition to the loss of my mother and the deaths of my aunt, Yudesi, and my brother, Langton, there were a number of other family deaths. In 1990, my father-in-law, Mr. Eriasafu Kyebakola, Mary's father, who stayed with us for a large portion of his later years, passed away at the age of ninety-six. He was a God-fearing man who, in his old age, volunteered to do daily maintenance at the Anglican cathedral until he lost his eyesight. He was also fond of reading his Bible every day. In 2003, my firstborn son, Moses Sembusi, an adventurous and intrepid young man with a great weakness for women, died, leaving us many grandchildren. Mary and I continue to take care of the younger ones. Through all the travails, Mary has been my rock and comforter; in this, she has only been superseded by God.

In 1993, Mary suffered a major stroke that paralyzed her right side. She was in a coma at Kitovu Catholic Hospital for over a month. We then transferred her to Mulago Hospital in Kampala, over ninety miles away, for more specialized treatment. She was hospitalized at Mulago for three months under the care of Dr. Kiryabirwe, a stroke specialist. By God's grace, Mary miraculously recovered and fully regained her faculties. We are very grateful to Dr. Kiryabirwe and the nurses for the great care they accorded her.

Mary has contributed a great deal to what I am today. She has supported me in my low moments and has also rejoiced with me in celebration of my achievements and successes. During our marriage, I have not been blemish free, but Mary has mercifully borne my weaknesses. Her love for me has enhanced my understanding of God's love for me. I could not have chosen a more suitable wife. Forgiveness, compassion, listening, and willingness to adjust to each other's peculiarities have also empowered our marriage.

Further, I believe that my acceptance of Jesus Christ as savior, dating back to August 9, 1959, has enabled me to adjust to his will and engendered the compassion, love, and understanding which have sustained us throughout our marriage.

Our Golden Jubilee celebrations fell on a Saturday, on December 28, 2013, at Namirembe Cathedral where we had gotten married exactly fifty years earlier. The bishop of Central Buganda Diocese, the Rt. Rev. Jackson Matovu, officiated at the jubilee service. Mary and I were very grateful to him; it was risky for him to accept given my current tenuous relationship with the church over LGBTQ issues.

The bishop sought permission from the incumbent archbishop, the Rt. Rev. Stanley Ntagali. And the archbishop graciously granted him the permission. Mary and I are grateful to the archbishop for opting not to treat us as renegades in God's church.

In addition to Bishop Matovu and his wife, other dignitaries at our anniversary celebration included former Katikkiro (prime minister of Buganda), the Hon. Dan Muliika; retired archbishop of the Church of Uganda, the Most Rev. Livingstone Mpalanyi Nkoyoyo and his wife; and my successor as bishop of West Buganda Diocese, the Rt. Rev. Kefa Semakula,[1] and his wife. The presence of the retired archbishop and bishops of the Church of Uganda was a manifestation of God's unconditional love.

During the service, our son, Timothy Mbaziira, read the first lesson, Genesis 2:18, 21–24: "Then the Lord God said, 'It is not good that the man should be alone; I will make him a helper as his partner.'" Indeed all of us, straight or gay, need the companionship and solidarity that marriage provides.

Our daughter, Mrs. Faith Nanyonjo Ntale, read the second reading, 1 Corinthians 13:1–13:

> Love is patient; love is kind; love is not envious or boastful or arrogant or rude. It does not insist on its own way; it is not irritable or resentful; it does not rejoice in wrongdoing, but rejoices in the truth. It bears all things, believes all things, hopes all things, endures all things. (vv. 4–7)

This reading was particularly pertinent in that therein lies a powerful prescription for a lasting marriage. The key ingredients of a successful marriage are patience, kindness, the containment of anger

---

1. Bishop Semakula has since retired.

and envy, forgiveness (keeping no record of wrongs), consideration (it is not self-seeking), trust, and communication. Mary and I have, by God's grace, attempted to live according to this prescription, *agape*, Greek for "unconditional love," attainable only through the grace of God.

Our friend, the Rev. Canon Prudence Kaddu, read the Gospel, Luke 4:18–19:

> The Spirit of the Lord is upon me,
>   because he has anointed me
>   to bring good news to the poor.
> He has sent me to proclaim release to the captives
>   and recovery of sight to the blind,
>   to let the oppressed go free,
> to proclaim the year of the Lord's favor.

We chose this reading purposely as an affirmation of the obligations of the ministry that God assigned to Mary and me during our long partnership: proclaiming good news to the poor, to prisoners, to the oppressed, and to the marginalized. Despite hardships, we have found that proclaiming God's Good News has strengthened our bond.

Following the church service, our children prepared for us a great reception which was expertly managed by a family friend, Mr. Solomon Rubondo, who served as the master of ceremonies. The celebration was filled with joy, recollection, merriment, and entertainment. It reminded me of Cana, without the wine! Mary is opposed to any kind of alcohol—she considers it the den of sin.

Over three hundred of our friends came to celebrate with us. I tell my children that friends come next to God and family. And that it is important to cultivate good friendships, which are often a bedrock of one's life. Indeed, next to God and my wife, my achievements and the person I am today are largely attributable to good friends.

To commemorate the occasion, our guests and children gave us many wonderful gifts. But what gratified us most was hearing our children talk about their appreciation of our sacrifices. They noted that we sent them to some of the finest schools despite less than stellar financial means. They also pointed out that our emphasis on daily prayer and on attending church services were foundational influences that shaped their lives. Mary and I were especially delighted when our grandchildren lauded our love for them. The little ones expressed their appreciation for the fun and food they enjoy and the gifts they get when they come to our home on special occasions such as Christmas and Easter.

These reminiscences highlighted the special role that parents play in the lives of children. Children closely observe their parents for cues on how to relate with others, on how to deal with conflict/adversity, and on how to celebrate life. It is important for parents to present a harmonious, united front. In his speech for the occasion, on behalf of all his siblings, Joseph noted that Mary and I always backed each other up while raising them. A united, harmonious front on issues is important because when children exploit loopholes in parents' resolve and outlook, discipline suffers. But a united front can only be achieved through constant communication, consultation, and in some cases, deference of primary decision-making responsibilities to either parent on certain issues. It is not always easy to be good role models for children, but by the grace of God, our children have turned out relatively well.

Invitation to Bless Roger and Casper's Wedding

I was recently reminded of the transcendental power of the bond of marriage when I was invited to sanctify Roger and Casper's wedding in Amsterdam, the Netherlands.[2]

In the evening of May 8, 2015, soon after my arrival in Amsterdam, Kim (the wedding coordinator), Roger, Casper, and I met to discuss the wedding service, which was scheduled for the following day. During our discussions, I discovered that Roger and Casper

---

2. Gay marriage is legal in the Netherlands, if one of the partners is a Dutch national or has residency.

were already legally married in both New York and in Amsterdam. My designated role was to confer God's blessing on their civil marriage. I was happy to note that Roger and Casper acknowledged that it is from God that everlasting love stems.

In the evening of May 9, 2015, invited guests boarded a boat on which the wedding ceremony took place. For the occasion, I chose to read the Scripture according to Mark 12:28–34:

> One of the scribes came near and heard them disputing with one another, and seeing that he answered them well, he asked him, "Which commandment is the first of all?" Jesus answered, "The first is, 'Hear, O Israel: the Lord our God, the Lord is one; you shall love the Lord your God with all your heart, and with all your soul, and with all your mind, and with all your strength.' The second is this, 'You shall love your neighbour as yourself.' There is no other commandment greater than these." (vv. 28–31)

In my remarks, I pointed out that the love of God is a wellspring from which unconditional love (*agape*) flows. Even though friendship (*filia*), affection (*storge*), and *eros* (romantic love) are important in any relationship, *agape* is the bedrock of any marriage. Without *agape*, couples may not endure the inevitable highs and lows (and occasional disappointments) that married people experience—in short, *agape* is the key to a lasting marriage.

I also pointed out that the beauty of God's creation is that each individual is unique and different. Consequently, in the course of their marriage, Roger and Casper would need to adjust to each other's uniqueness and difference.

After I blessed the rings, the couple exchanged vows, placed the rings on each other's fingers, and kissed; it was a joyous occasion. I was honored and happy to be invited to participate in sanctifying Roger's and Casper's marriage.

My participation in the ceremony was one of the high points of my service to the LGBTQ community thus far. It affirmed my conviction that God's love is inclusive of all people.

Concluding Thoughts on Love, Peace, and Justice in the World

AS I CONCLUDE THE ACCOUNT of my work in God's ministry thus far, I would like to highlight some of the Bible verses that have sustained me and which I believe to hold the key to a more peaceful and just world.

Love

God's primary commandment to us is to love one another as he loves us. 1 John 4:7–9 says:

> Beloved, let us love one another, because love is from God; every-one who loves is born of God and knows God. Whoever does not love does not know God, for God is love. God's love was revealed among us in this way: God sent his only Son into the world so that we might live through him.

And 1 Corinthians 13:4–7 reads:

> Love is patient; love is kind; love is not envious or boastful or arrogant or rude. It does not insist on its own way; it is not irri-table or resentful; it does not rejoice in wrongdoing, but rejoices in the truth. It bears all things, believes all things, hopes all things, endures all things.

And finally Mark 12:30–31 tells us:

> "'You shall love the Lord your God with all your heart, and with all your soul, and with all your mind, and with all your strength.' The

second is this, 'You shall love your neighbour as yourself.' There is no other commandment greater than these."

Love transcends envy, jealousy, fear, and mistrust. If we truly loved our neighbors as we love ourselves, there would be no wars; we would not discriminate against each other on the basis of race, gender, culture, or sexual orientation; we would not countenance extreme poverty and depravation; and we would stand up to injustice wherever it appears. Our love should be unconditional, as is God's love for us, for he gave his only son to die for our sins in spite of our inequities. Our priority as Christians made in the image of God should be to advocate for the infusion of love into world politics and institutions.

Forgiveness

Daniel 9:9–10 states:

> To the Lord our God belong mercy and forgiveness, for we have rebelled against him, and have not obeyed the voice of the Lord our God by following his laws, which he set before us by his servants the prophets.

Through Jesus, the Lord forgives our sins and trespasses. In order to walk in God's path, we ought to forgive others for wrongs they do to us. The endless wars in the world are a result of the lack of love and forgiveness.

As we read in 1 Corinthians 13:5, love does not keep a record of wrongs; in order to love our neighbors as ourselves, we need to be able to forgive. Forgiveness frees our souls, and allows us to exhibit God's love unencumbered.

Reconciliation

Without forgiveness, there can be no reconciliation. Second Corinthians 5:17–21 tells us:

So if anyone is in Christ, there is a new creation: everything old has passed away; see, everything has become new! All this is from God, who reconciled us to himself through Christ, and has given us the ministry of reconciliation; that is, in Christ God was reconciling the world to himself, not counting their trespasses against them, and entrusting the message of reconciliation to us. So we are ambassadors for Christ, since God is making his appeal through us; we entreat you on behalf of Christ, be reconciled to God. For our sake he made him to be sin who knew no sin, so that in him we might become the righteousness of God.

Forgiveness gives us the pathway to reconciliation. And through reconciliation, "the old has gone, the new is here." Indeed, reconciliation enabled my ministry in West Buganda Diocese to proceed peacefully. Likewise, in our lives and in politics, reconciliation allows us to supersede any past wrongs or grievances. Nelson Mandela's example in South Africa is a good illustration of the power of reconciliation.

Faith and Prayer

Philippians 4:4–7 tells us:

Rejoice in the Lord always; again I will say, Rejoice. Let your gentleness be known to everyone. The Lord is near. Do not worry about anything, but in everything by prayer and supplication with thanksgiving let your requests be made known to God. And the peace of God, which surpasses all understanding, will guard your hearts and your minds in Christ Jesus.

Faith in God and putting all one's concerns to the Lord in prayer are the bedrock of a Christian's life. Whatever hardships and obstacles have come my way, I have found that my faith in God has always calmed me. If you have faith, all you need to do is to pray to Him, and leave the rest to Him. The Lord is our comfort and strength (Ps. 23:4).

I am optimistic that despite the dark forces of evil in the world today, the God of love shall not allow a devilish empire to rule his people. Isaiah 58:11 assures that:

> The LORD will guide you continually,
>> and satisfy your needs in parched places,
>> and make your bones strong;
> and you shall be like a watered garden,
>> like a spring of water,
>> whose waters never fail.

I pray that the Lord guides the world's authorities into the path of love, justice, compassion, and forgiveness.

In conclusion, I thank God for enabling me to serve him and for the many blessings and honors he has granted me while in his service. I am also grateful that God has enabled me to witness and to appreciate the diversity of his creation as I give testimony to Christ's Good News in various countries of the world.

Concerned Christian's E-mail to the Archbishop on the LGBT Controversy

Mayanja Kizito John, 3rd April 2006
(E-mail address and phone number omitted)

The Archbishop of
The Church of Uganda

Your Grace,

RE: Expelling Rt. Rev. Dr. Christopher Ssenyonjo Followed Wrong Procedure

I have prayerfully considered this issue, I have also discussed with some senior clergy in the Church of Uganda, I have carefully studied relevant scriptures and I have arrived at a conclusion that your attempt to stop Rt. Rev. Dr. Christopher Ssenyonjo from exercising his pastoral duties as a bishop in the Church of Uganda is not only administrative wrong, but also contradicts the Holy Scriptures (Matthew 18:15–17).

1. I have observed that you and other bishops in the Church of Uganda have deliberately decided to misrepresent Bishop Ssenyonjo. He is not promoting gayism/lesbianism. He is only providing minorities and other social outcasts with pastoral care just in the same way Jesus welcomed them like the lepers, prostitutes, women, children, tax collectors and all sorts of sinners. It was the religious leaders of the time (Pharisees) who used to condemn him (Luke 7:39). These religious leaders eventually made the plan that led to his crucifixion.

I see a lot of similarities between Bishop Ssenyonjo and Jesus Christ. I also see in him characteristics of St. Paul, especially Paul's advocating for the inclusion of the uncircumcised in the early church. Bishop Ssenyonjo has taken a bold decision similar to that of St. Peter of dining with sinners (the uncircumcised) (Acts 11:3).

2. I find it very strange for His Grace to use a populist approach of excommunicating his brother bishop in the press. For the Christian principles of helping a brother who has gone astray (I do not believe Bishop Ssenyonjo has) are clearly laid down in Matthew 18:15–17. In my understanding it is

only the House of Bishops or the Provincial Assembly that would advise the Archbishop what to do with his errant brother.

In case there was need to take urgent measures to address any damage to the church of Uganda (if there was any), a confidential pastoral letter addressed to all bishops and to Bishop Ssenyonjo would suffice.

Don't you feel guilty my Lord that the whole issue is now being trivialized; instead of condemning Bishop Ssenyonjo for breaking off from the church of Uganda, he is being condemned for being a pro-Gay bishop? Is this the reason you decided to expel him from the church? If so why did you choose to do it at this point in time and not earlier?

Don't you think, my Lord, you can learn from the way the Roman Catholic Church handles problems that crop up in her church? Compare the way they handled the issue of the bishop who got married! Could this be one of the reasons why the Roman Catholic clergy have kept their dignity and the Church remained united?

I need some advice my Lord, for I have overheard a number of people discussing some scandals which are totally in conflict with the Biblical teachings done by serving bishops in the Church of Uganda! Should these be openly condemned in the press also?

Don't you think you have invited the laity to ridicule the clergy and will not only stop at Bishop Ssenyonjo! You have just opened the Pandora box[sic]! Your action is not very different from your predecessor who single handedly reversed the decision of the House of Bishops, which had appointed Rev. Canon Maguzi as Bishop of West Buganda Diocese! This meant that there are times when the House of Bishops is guided by something else other than the Holy Spirit. Such a precedent could be responsible for the current Muhabura crisis. Let the Church of Uganda be prepared for more! In my opinion exposing weakness of senior church leaders [is] tantamount to bringing shame to the whole body of Christ!

3. My Lord, I think you have shunned away from the real pastoral needs of the people of Uganda/God and have opted for soft targets. Gayism/lesbianism is not a big problem in Uganda, and if the clergy do not give it publicity, very few people would even know that Bishop Ssenyonjo has them as his clients. In fact heterosexuals have caused more problems in Uganda. They have defiled babies, raped old women, sexually harassed women in offices and at church altars, have produced and abandoned children who move to the streets, have had sex (beastiality) with pigs, dogs, cows, hens, have spread HIV/AIDS, etc. These are some of the issues that need/call for your urgent attention!

4. I have not come across in church history church leaders who have done their pastoral work properly and remained popular with governments! Indeed Archbishop Janan Luwum paid the real price! He was never praised the way your actions are praised by government spokespersons! I highly doubt whether these government spokesperson and laity have capacity to critically analyze theological issues you have brought to them!

Ugandans need to know the Church of Uganda's stand on the war in the north, poverty, human rights violations, corruption, etc. We only hear a lonely voice—the Roman Catholic Church. Why is the Church of Uganda not responding to people's social needs just like the Roman Catholic Church does?

5. Correct me if I am wrong my Lord, but none of us is righteous before God (Roman 3:9–12). I wonder whether there is still any bishop in the Church of Uganda today (who have done so many unholy things to reach those positions) with the moral authority to condemn others? Jesus told us not to judge others (Mathew 7:1–5).

I personally have a case of theft against the Church of Uganda. My father worked as a Lay Reader for 10 years and church leaders in Namirembe Diocese ate his pension. Those thieves also need to be excommunicated.

Why does the Church of Uganda not consider some of Bishop Ssenyonjo's strength! I am one of those who has been happily married for 16 years and I attribute this to the good choice I made after reading Bishop Ssenyonjo's book on marriage—"*Ssenyonjo C (1982), Choosing a Partner Centenary Publishing House Ltd, Kampala.*" I also think that many clergy in the Church of Uganda would not have been what they are if it was not because of Bishop Ssenyonjo's liberal attitude! Bishop Ssenyonjo is an excellent counselor whose services are badly needed in the Church of Uganda.

In my opinion the Church of Uganda should have carefully considered his views and if found them too controversial in Uganda, they should have persuaded him to take them to another church in the Anglican communion instead of condemning him.

6. Lastly I think it is good manners to have respect for elders. Bishop Ssenyonjo is a senior clergy, who has served as a bishop for 24 years and was the Dean of the Province of the Church of Uganda. He is well read, calm and approachable. He has a family and I am sure, as a human being, has feelings. Even if he was in the wrong, he deserves to be corrected in a more dignified manner!

However, I am always amazed by the way he reacts when he is hurt. I have never heard him condemning those who condemn him. He is a real sacrificial lamb. My prayer is that God you hasten to: fulfill thy word in Romans 12:17–21. Amen.

I remain your Lordship's faithful servant,

MAYANJA KIZITO JOHN

Appendix 1B

Marble Nabbumba Kijjambu
(Phone number and e-mail address omitted)

21st June 2007

Your Grace,
The Archbishop of the Province of the Church of Uganda
Kampala

I greet you in the name of the Lord Jesus Christ.

The coming of Christ was the message that could be the pillar of the church, thus "Repent ye for the Kingdom of God is at hand."

Your Grace the Archbishop of the Anglican Province of the Church of Uganda; I appreciate your distastefulness towards homosexuality. However, I hold a different approach towards fighting the issue. You should be aware that the problem is already here in Uganda and more so, in the church you lead.

Historians will agree with me your Grace, that homosexuality was here before the coming of Europeans in our beloved palaces. It is also historically evident that homosexuality existed in the once famous Bishop Tucker Theological College among tutors and students. Your Grace right here in Uganda there is a famous secondary school, which I am not disclosing, after finding out the practice amidst the students, resolved to expel them.

However, later they found out that this was no solution they decided to identify the primary schools from which those students come. They identified them and decided not to admit pupils from those schools.

However, Your Grace this was neither solution nor a treatment to the problem.

I have even witnessed a person in Jesus' committee in a training school who testified to have been a lesbian.

Your Grace the problem of Gays is amidst our society, more so this generation of my children your grandchildren, so as we should not behave like ostriches, we must face it other than running away from it.

We should face realities of life as Jesus did when he confronted those who had turned the temple into a market place or even at crucifixion he never ran away.

As a parent I am in tears for not being certain whether my own children are gays. As a member of Mothers Union, where one of our duties is to bring up our children in a God fearing manner, I am concerned that the gays are existing and living with my Children.

I have prayed for long over this issue and after prayer and fasting, I am convinced that the Holy Spirit has directed me to write to you this message. The Holy Spirit is telling me that the method you have decided to use to fight gays lacks in Godly standards.

His worship the Archbishop, it was in February 2007 when you made touching news by refusing to partake Holy Communion during an Anglican Primates Summit in Tanzania. Your Grace the Bible and theology teaches that the sacraments turn pure despite the celebrants then why did you deny the Holy Spirit?

Then this May 2007, at your residence at Namirembe, while addressing the press, you were quoted by one local Newspaper to have said, "We have decided that if the American bishops are invited, the bishops of the Church of Uganda are not going," thus boycotting the Lambeth Conference. Jesus dined with sinners, then you, who is leading the Church of Uganda, to refuse the steps of Christ are you developing another salvation method other than that you preach? During your recent Mukono tour, you urged students to study theology. Theology is not applied in your church, and then why should they study it?

I have witnessed many other incidents even read in the papers that your method in dealing with homosexuals and lesbians is either by boycotting or excommunicating those who hold different views from yours.

Your Grace, I hold a different approach on this issue. I may be certain that after reading this message, you are going to excommunicate me from my church as you did to Bishop Christopher Senyonjo. Know this your Grace that excommunicating people or not attending conferences is not and will never be a solution to this problem.

St. Paul in 1Cor 12:5 agrees that, we may differ in administration but we are one body. So by cutting off some posts, let it be an individual, or a group as you do, by not attending meetings, etc., is not spiritual.

What will you explain to the Lord as to why you hated people he gave you to care for? 1 John 2:9 disagrees with people who say, "They are in light and hate their brothers, that they are in darkness even until now."

What surprises me, your Grace, is how you go on giving testimonies that you were a drunkard, a womanizer, a smoker, etc., and the Lord saved you from those things as it appeared in one of the local Luganda daily. Then had you been disowned by whoever preached to you, would you have been saved? Or had the church excommunicated you would you have ever been a bishop?

I see hypocrisy in all this. Jesus in Luke 11:46 condemned hypocritical behavior of those who called themselves defenders of the system by then. He said *"Woe unto you also, ye lawyers. For ye lade men with burdens grievous to be borne, and you yourselves touch not the burdens with one of your fingers."*

Your Grace the burden you are telling others to lift is too heavy. Think again.

Drunkards, womanizers, smokers, homosexuals, hypocrites, thieves, etc., are all saved by Grace, not by humans. Don't judge others so that you are not judged.

Yours,
Marble Nabbumba Kijjambu

c.c. All Bishops
c.c. Interested parties

Appendix 2

Awards and Compliments

1983

Doctor of Divinity (Hon.), Berkeley Divinity School, Yale University

1994

King's College Budo,

Order of Merit—Christopher Senyonjo

An old Budonian (1947–1952) has this day been awarded the Order of Merit for distinguished service to the nation signed by the President, the Secretary and one member of the United Budonian's Club.

March 26, 1994

1996

American Biographical Institute—**Gold Record of Achievement**, 1996

Awarded to Bishop Christopher Senyonjo in honor of career excellence and outstanding contributions to International Society.

2010

The International Jose Julo Samia Award

Presented to Bishop Christopher Senyonjo

Signed: City Commissioner, Nicole Murray Ramirez, Executive Director International Council, USA—Canada—Mexico

May 19, 2010

City of San Diego—Human Relations Commission
Special Commendation

Bishop Christopher Senyonjo

Signed: Nicole Murray Ramirez, Human Relations Commissioner, May 19, 2010

For Gospel witness to the full inclusion of all people and standing
courageously for human rights and dignity

May 24, 2010

The Center for Lesbian and Gay Studies in Religion and Ministry
recognizes and honors

The Rt. Rev. Christopher Senyonjo

as a leading voice

signed on this 24th day of May 2010

Bernard Schlayer, PhD, Executive Director, the Center for Lesbian and Gay
Studies in Religion and Ministry at Pacific School of Religion

June 2010

In honor of Bishop Christopher Senyonjo

For compassionate advocacy

of human rights worldwide

From your grateful friends in

Orange County, CA

June 2010

2011

2011 UNITAS VERITAS AWARD UNION THEOLOGICAL SEMINARY
in the City of New York

Proudly honors

Distinguished alumnus The Rt. Rev. Bishop Christopher Senyonjo—'66, '67

Bishop, counselor, activist, devoted servant leader, and human rights
advocate for global equality; for your courageous advocacy on the part of
LGBT persons in Uganda and worldwide; for embodying the heart of God
with gentle compassion, and radical inclusive love for all creation; and for
modeling what an active faith requires for us to do justice, to love kindness,
and to walk humbly with our God

Awarded this Fourteenth day of October 2011, Serene Jones, President

2012

June 2012

BRC—Bayard Rustin Coalition

Fighting for Black LGBT Equality since 2006

Global Grand Marshal

Bishop Christopher Senyonjo

For his courageous leadership in the advancement of global equality and human rights for all

September 2012

The Clinton Global Initiative

2012 CLINTON GLOBAL CITIZEN AWARD

On September 24, 2012

December 2012

State of California Senate

Certificate of Recognition

Bishop Christopher Senyonjo

In recognition of your outstanding leadership and courage to end

Harassment and discrimination

of Lesbian, Gay, Bisexual, Transgender people in Uganda and the United States

December 2, 2012

Christine Kehoe, 39th District

Appendix 3

Clergy I Ordained

The following are the names of the clergy that I have been able to ordain:
(1) Rev. Godfrey Makumbi, (2) Rev. Samuel Mwesigwa, (3) Rev. Christopher Ssensalo, (4) Rev. David Kamwanyi, (5) Rev. Samuel Mukasa, (6) Rev. Charles Kato Mukundi, (7) Rev. L. Mukasa, (8) Rev. George Musharanga, (9) Rev. E. Luzzi Kirumira, (10) Rev. S. Muwonge, (11) Rev. S. Ssali, (12) Rev. Elia Paul Kamasajja, (13) Rev. Y. Salli Wasswa, (14) Rev. D. L. Mutabaluka, (15) Rev. D. Serujoba, (16) Rev. Y. Kimera, (17) Rev. Edward Lubega, (18) Rev. Christopher Musisi, (19) Rev. Paul Mulindwa, (20) Rev. Duncan Luyinda, (21) Rev. S. Muteesasira, (22) Rev. I. Kijjambu, (23) Rev. Yoram Lubega, (24) Rev. Beatrice Kyobe, (25) Rev. Moses Katuteyo, (26) Rev. George Walakira, (27) Rev. Paul Ruzindana, (28) Rev. Willy Mwesigwa, (29) Rev. Winfred Mwine, (30) Rev. Christopher Bbale, (31) Rev. Eria Kayemba, (32) Rev. Tabitha N. Dembe, (33) Rev. Johnson Ndyamuba, (34) Rev. Enock Muhanguzi, (35) Rev. Herbert Tumwine, (36) Rev. Wilson Bahitana, (37) Rev. Eric Nsubuga, (38) Rev. James Bananuka, (39) Rev. Stephen Mujuni, (40) Rev. Eric N. Lukooko, (41) Rev. Eric Tumuhairwe, (42) Rev. Alfred Mwesigye, (43) Rev. Charles Turyagumanawe, (44) Rev. G. Rwantani Birondwa, (45) Rev. Richard Kagimu, (46) Rev. Stephen JJunju, (47) Rev. Ezra Tumusime, (48) Rev. Charles W. Nsubuga, (49) Rev. Ham Mwesigwa, (50) Rev. John Kamuhanda, (51) Rev. Emmanuel Tumwesigye, (52) Rev. Patrick Ndhuyi, (53) Rev. Emmanuel Tumwesigye, (54) Rev. Patrick Ndhuyi, (55) Rev. Sam Benon Ddungu, (56) Rev. James Njemia, (57) Rev. David Tamale, (58) Rev. Charles Muhairwe, (59) Rev. Enock Katojo, (60) Rev. Charles Matovu, (61) Rev. Juliet N. Rebecca Nantongo, (62) Rev. Robert Ndyabalema, (63) Rev. John Kakooza, (64) Rev. E. K. Tibeijuka, (65) Rev. William Muchyakumba, (66) Rev. Christopher Muwonge, (67) Rev. Stephen Kakuru, (68) Rev. Enock Ssebuliba, (69) Rev. Ssonko Kimbowa, (70) Rev. Nimrod Ssekamatte, (71) Rev. G. Kitimbo, (72) Rev. Isaac Nsereko, (73) Rev. Kakowe Kowe Wamala, (74) Rev. Charles Mugisha, (75) Rev. David Lweyisa, (76) Rev. Edward Kayemba, (77) Rev. Edward Kambugu, (78) Rev. Justine Muwanga, (79) Rev. Cranmer Ssempebwa, (80) Rev. Francis Kakooza, (81) Rev. Paul Mbaziira, (82) Rev. Stephen Mulindwa,

(83) Rev. John Turyamureeba, (84) Rev. Livingstone Serunjogi, (85) Rev. Kibuuka Bbosa, (86) Rev. Polycarp Lubowa, (87) Rev. Isaaya Mugerwa, (88) Rev. James G. Arinaitwe, (89) Rev. Jackson R. S. Kusasira, (90) Rev. William Busulwa, (91) Rev. Paul Busulwa, (92) Rev. Charles J. Kafeero, (93) Rev. Godfrey M. Kasiita, (94) Rev. Borad Matovu, (95) Rev. Nathan Wamala, (96) Rev. Gladys Namukwaya, (97) Rev. George William Lubega, (98) Rev. Charles Kalema, (99) Rev. Davis Byanyima, (100) Rev. Daniel Kasagga, (101) Rev. Charles Gumisiriza, (102) Rev. Esther F. Lutaya, (103) Rev. Ezekiel Mawanda, (104) Rev. Erone A. Zawedde, (105) Rev. David Livingstone Mutabaluka, (106) Rev. John Patrick Rwabigonji, (107) Rev. Stanley Ndawula, (108) Rev. Robert Kintu Kalyango, (109) Rev. Christopher Bafirawala, (110) Rev. Gordon Kasagga, (111) Rev. John Kakoza, (112) Rev. Yekoyada K. Matovu, (113) Rev. Kopuliano Nsubuga, (114) Rev. Patrick Kamuni, (115) Rev. Benson Agaba, (116) Rev. Fredrick Sseremba, (117) Rev. Paul Sekweyama, (118) Rev. Molly Nuwagaba, (119) Rev. Florence Namala, (120) Rev. Christopher Rwakanga, (121) Rev. Jane N. Babirye, (122) Rev. Stanley Gumisiriza, (123) Rev. James Ruhiriga, (124) Rev. Nathan Nkiriirwa, (125) Rev. Joseph Mugerwa, (126) Rev. George W. Ndawula, (127) Rev. Isaac Biri-eri-Mukama, (128) Rev. John F. Kamuntu, (129) Rev. Jackson Kasozi Nsamba, (130) Rev. Nathan Kasozi, (131) Rev. Byamugisha, (132) Rev. Godfrey Mpuuga, (133) Rev. Godfrey Kosea Mugabi, (134) Rev. Kayiwa Lule, (135) Rev. David Lubulwa, (136) Rev. Katerega Bakubanja, (137) Rev. John Kyeyune, (138) Rev. Eria Sekyondwa, (139) Rev. Revison Mukasa, (140) Rev. Davis Kasenge, (141) Rev. Eliezer Katongole, (142) Rev. Frederick Kibuka, (143) Rev. Nathan Mbuga, (144) Rev. John William Mukuye, (145) Rev. Francis Kapere, (146) Rev. James Muliika, (147) Rev. Juliet Ssanyu Kewaza, (148) Rev. Cranmer Kabanga Kizza, (149) Rev. Godfrey Nawejje, (150) Rev. Frederick John Lwebuga, (151) Rev. Sam Baker Sango Senkindu, (152) Rev. Yekoyada Kimera, (153) Rev. Moses Kabigumira, (154) Rev. Jackson Mugisha, (155) Rev. J. W. Ssali, (156) Rev. B. Kasamba, (157) Rev. Benon Mugisha, (158) Rev. C. Zavuga Lubega, (159) Rev. Eliya Paul Kayiira, (160) Rev. George Kayiira, (161) Rev. Harriet Nambuusi, (162) Rev. George W. Muyomba, (163) Rev. Samuel Kayima, (164) Rev. James Kazalwa, (165) Rev. Godfrey Kasagga, (166) Rev. Knaack Jasper Kyeyune, (167) Rev. Abel N Katunguka, (168) Rev. Charles Tukamuhabwa, (169) Rev. Eriazali Sentamu, (170) Rev. Francis Kakooza, (171) Rev. John Kiyemba, (172) Rev. Kezlon Kiwanuka, (173) Rev. Sam Sengendo, (174) Rev. Erias Muhamba, (175) Rev. Dan Ddumba, (176) Rev. Nyanzi E., (177) Rev. Shadrack Kiwuwa, (178) Rev. Benon Mubiru, (179) Rev. David Mubiru, (180) Rev. Ignatius

Kaziringa, (181) Rev. Justine Kiwanuka, (182) Rev. John Nandabi, (183) Rev. G. Katalemwa, (184) Rev. Ssekitoleko, (185) Rev. F. W. Ssemanda, (186) Rev. John Nandabi, (187) Rev. Yowasi Namuyenga, (188) Rev. Mary Tusuubira, (189) Rev. Jonathan Nsubuga, (190) Rev. L. S. Musembwa, (191) Rev. E. Ndugwa, (192) Rev. L. S. Musembwa, (193) Rev. Edward F. Serubugo, (194) Rev. C. B. Nsubuga, (195) Rev. Jafessi Kaweesa, (196) Rev. Christine Namukasa, (197) Rev. Patrick Kalanzi, (198) Rev. Yasam Kyomya, (199) Rev. Fred Kanakulya, (200) Rev. C. B. Namugera, (201) Rev. D. J. Jjemba, (202) Rev. William Mukuye, (203) Rev. Misaeri Musoke, (204) Rev. Martin Kiwanuka, (205) Rev. Nathan Kashaija, (206) Rev. James Kabweine, (207) Rev. Erasmus Nsamba, (208) Rev. Proscovia Semanda, (209) Rev. Mutawe, (210) Rev. Samuel Tusuubira, (211) Rev. Festo Ssali, (212) Rev. J. Sekakozi, (213) Rev. S. K. Kiwumulo, (214) Rev. Wasswa-Ssentamu, (215) Rev. Amos Kasibante, (216) Rev. Erisa Grace Sentongo, (217) Rev. Abias Kibirige, (218) Rev. Stephen Kewaza, (219) Rev. James Kabanda, (220) Rev. L. Mayambala, (221) Rev. Winnie Nuwagaba Namara, (222) Rev. Samuel Kabogoza, (223) Rev. S. Luzibona

Appendix 4

List of Countries I Have Visited Doing God's Ministry

Uppsala and Stockholm, **Sweden**

Rome, **Italy**

Paris, **France**

Vancouver, Victoria Island, Ottawa, and Saint John, **Canada**

Glasgow and Edinburgh, **Scotland**

Dubai, **United Arab Emirates**

London, Ipswich, Bristol, Salisbury, Lambeth, Manchester, Brighton, Cambridge, **England**

Nairobi, Mombasa, Nakuru, Kisumu, and Eldoret, **Kenya**

Dar es Salaam, Bukoba, Arusha, and Moshi, **Tanzania**

Kigali and Gisenyi, **Rwanda**

Bujumbura, **Burundi**

Bukavu, **Democratic Republic of the Congo**

Yei, **South Sudan**

Lilongwe, **Malawi**

Harare, **Zimbabwe**

United States: New York, **New York**; Washington, DC; Cleveland, **Ohio**; Denver, **Colorado**; Newark, **New Jersey**; Los Angeles, Palm Springs, San Francisco, San Diego, Sacramento, **California**; Jacksonville, **Florida**; Las Vegas, **Nevada**; Indianapolis, **Indiana**; Boston and Cambridge, **Massachusetts**; Chicago, **Illinois**; Atlanta, **Georgia**; Portland, **Oregon**; Minneapolis, Duluth, and St. Paul, **Minnesota**; Memphis, **Tennessee**; Hartford and New Haven, **Connecticut**; Salt Lake City and Park City, **Utah**; Boise, **Idaho**; Providence, **Rhode Island**; New Orleans, **Louisiana**

Dublin and Belfast, **Ireland**

Seoul and Busan, **South Korea**

Tel Aviv and Jerusalem, **Israel**
Johhanesberg, Cape Town, Pretoria, **South Africa**
Bombay (Mumbai), **India**
Mexico City, **Mexico**
Brisbane, Sydney, Canberra, and Melbourne, **Australia**
Amsterdam, **Netherlands**

Appendix 5

Photos

Silver jubilee photograph.

Namirembe Cathedral, the mother cathedral of the Anglican Church of Uganda, where:

1. I became a deacon in 1963
2. we got married in 1963
3. I became a vicar in 1968

4. I was consecrated as bishop in 1974
5. we celebrated our Golden Jubilee marriage anniversary in 2013.

Photograph taken at Mityana Cathedral in 1977, after the reconciliation service for Bishop Festo Lutaya.

CPSIA information can be obtained
at www.ICGtesting.com
Printed in the USA
LVOW01s1933240516
489772LV00005B/7/P